National Standards

for

History

for

Grades K-4

Expanding Children's World in Time and Space

**Expanded Edition
Including Examples of
Student Achievement
for Grades K-2 and 3-4**

National Center for History in the Schools

University of California, Los Angeles

The development of the National Standards for History for Grades K-4 was administered by the National Center for History in the Schools at the University of California, Los Angeles under the guidance of the National Council for History Standards. The standards were developed with funding from the National Endowment for the Humanities and the U.S. Department of Education. This publication does not necessarily represent positions or policies of the United States government, and no official endorsement should be inferred. With the exception of photographs and other visual materials, this publication may be freely reproduced and distributed for educational and research purposes.

Project Co-directors: Charlotte Crabtree
                                  Gary B. Nash

Project Assistant Director: Linda Symcox

Art Director: Robin Weisz

Production planning: Chris Coniglio

Production: UCLA Publication Design Services

Document control: Marta Hill

Copyright procurement: Leticia Zermeno

First Printing 1994

Ordering Information

National Standards for History for Grades K-4
ISBN 0-9633218-3-8

Write to:

National Center for History in the Schools
University of California, Los Angeles
10880 Wilshire Blvd., Suite 761
Los Angeles, CA 90024-4108
FAX: (310) 825-4723

PREFACE

Publication of the *National Standards for History for Grades K-4* could not be more timely. These standards address one of the major goals for education reform contained in the landmark legislation, **Goals 2000: Educate America Act,** signed into law by President Bill Clinton in March 1994. This statute affirms that by the year 2000, "All students will leave grades 4, 8, and 12 having demonstrated competency over challenging subject matter" in the core academic subjects of the school curriculum, history among them. Heralding passage of this legislation by the Congress, Secretary of Education Richard W. Riley announced, "Final passage of the Goals 2000 legislation moves us one step closer to the day when we can assure every parent in America that their children . . . are receiving an education that is up to world class standards." It is a goal broadly supported by the American people, their state governors, their legislators in the United States Congress, and the successive administrations of Presidents George Bush and Bill Clinton.

Support for the development of internationally competitive national standards of excellence for the nation's schools was first voiced in the National Education Goals adopted by the nation's fifty governors in their 1989 meeting in Charlottesville, Virginia. The third of the six education goals adopted in that meeting identified history as one of five school subjects for which challenging new national achievement standards should be established.

In October 1992 President Clinton reaffirmed his commitment to achieving these goals, including the "establishment of world class standards [specifically to include history] and development of a meaningful national examination system . . . to determine whether our students are meeting the standards . . . , to increase expectations, and to give schools incentives and structures to improve student performance." That same year, the importance of national standards in history was again affirmed in *Raising Standards for American Education*, the report to Congress of the National Council on Education Standards and Testing, appointed by the Congress to advise on these matters under the co-chairmanship of Governors Roy Romer (D-Colorado) and Carroll A. Campbell (R-South Carolina).

It was in this robust climate of education reform that the National History Standards Project was born. Funded in the spring of 1992 by the National Endowment for the Humanities and the Office of Educational Research and Improvement of the United States Department of Education, this Project sought to develop broad national consensus for what constitutes excellence in the teaching and learning of history in the nation's schools. Developed through a broad-based national consensus-building process, this task has involved working toward agreement both on the larger purposes of history in the school curriculum and on the more specific history understandings and thinking processes all students should have equal opportunity to acquire over twelve years of precollegiate education.

In undertaking this process, it was widely agreed that the History Standards, as finally drafted, would mark a critical advance but not the final destination in what must be an ongoing, dynamic process of improvement and revision over the years to come. History is an extraordinarily dynamic field today, and standards drafted for the schools must be open to continuing development to keep pace with new refinements and revisions in this field.

This present publication, *National Standards for History for Grades K-4*, marks a major milestone in the development of standards of excellence for the nation's schools. It is the result of over two years of intensive work by gifted classroom teachers of history; of supervisors, state social studies specialists, and chief state school officers responsible for history in the schools; of talented and active academic historians in the nation; and of representatives of a broad array of professional and scholarly organizations, civic and public interest groups, parents and individual citizens with a stake in the teaching of history in the schools.

The National Council for History Standards, the policy-setting body responsible for providing policy direction and oversight of the Project, consisted of 30 members, including the present or immediate past presidents of such large-membership organizations directly responsible for the content and teaching of history as the Council of Chief State School Officers, the Association for Supervision and Curriculum Development, the Council of State Social Studies Specialists, the National Council for the Social Studies, the Organization of American Historians, the National Council for History Education, and the Organization of History Teachers. In addition, members included the director and associate director of the Social Studies Development Center at Indiana University, supervisory and curriculum development staff of county and city school districts, experienced classroom teachers, and distinguished historians in the fields of United States and world history. To foster correspondence in the development of these standards with the work under development for the 1994 National Assessment of Educational Progress (NAEP) in United States History, several participants in the NAEP Planning and Steering Committees were included in the National Council for History Standards. For similar reasons two members of the Congressionally-mandated National Council for Education Standards and Testing also served on this Council. Finally, the two directors of the National Center for History in the Schools, responsible for administering this Project, served as co-chairs of the Council.

The National Forum for History Standards was composed of representatives from major education, public interest, parent-teacher, and other organizations concerned with history in the schools. Advisory in its function, the Forum provided important counsel and feedback for this project as well as access to the larger public through the membership of the organizations represented in the Forum.

Nine Organizational Focus Groups of between 15 and 29 members each, chosen by the leadership of their respective organizations, were engaged to provide important advisory, review, and consulting services to the project. Organizations providing this special service included the Council of Chief State School Officers, the Association for Supervision and Curriculum Development, the American Historical Association, the World History Association, the National Council for the Social Studies, the Organization of American Historians, the National Council for History Education, the Council of State Social Studies Specialists, and the Organization of History Teachers.

Three Curriculum Task Forces were formed, totaling more than 50 members, with responsibility for developing the standards for students in grades kindergarten through four, and for students in grades five through twelve in the fields of United States and world history. Composed of veteran classroom teachers from throughout the United States who had been recommended by the many organizations participating in this Project, and of recognized scholars of United States and world history with deep commitments to history education in schools, these groups have worked for many months in grade-alike writing teams and in meetings of the whole to ensure continuity of standards across all levels of schooling, elementary through high school.

The Appendix presents the rosters of all these working groups. Deep appreciation is owed to every one of these participants, all of whom gave unfailingly and selflessly of their time and professional expertise during the more than two years of intensive work that went into the development, recurrent national reviews, revisions, and final editorial refinements of this volume. In particular we express deep appreciation to Sara Shoob, Cub Run Elementary School, Centreville, Virginia, who chaired the Curriculum Task Force for the K-4 History Standards; and to Helen Debelak, Birchwood Elementary and Junior High School, Cleveland, Ohio and John M.

Fisher, Fifth Avenue Elementary School, Columbus, Ohio, who served with Shoob as the editorial team who responded to the recommendations of all the review groups and worked long hours throughout the late spring and summer months of 1994 to refine the standards and bring them to completion.

Special appreciation is due, also, to the many thousands of teachers, curriculum leaders, assessment experts, historians, parents, textbook publishers, and others too numerous to mention who have sought review copies of the standards and turned out for public hearings and information sessions scheduled at regional and national conferences throughout these two years, and who have provided their independent assessments and recommendations for making these Standards historically sound, workable in classrooms, and responsive to the needs and interests of students in the schools.

Finally, we note with appreciation the funding provided by the National Endowment for the Humanities and by the Office of Educational Research and Improvement of the United States Department of Education to conduct this complex and broadly inclusive enterprise.

In this most contentious field of the curriculum, there have been many who have wondered if a national consensus could be forged concerning what all students should have opportunity to learn about the history of their nation and the world, and of the peoples of all racial, religious, ethnic, and national backgrounds who have been a part of that story. The responsiveness, enormous good will, and dogged determination of so many to meet this challenge has reinforced our confidence in the inherent strength and capabilities of this nation now to undertake the steps necessary for bringing to all students the benefits of this endeavor. The stakes are high. It is the challenge that must now be undertaken.

Charlotte Crabtree and Gary B. Nash
Co-directors

Photograph by Leslie Slavin
Courtesy of the American Association
of School Librarians/ALA

Abraham Lincoln with son, Tad. Library of Congress

TABLE OF CONTENTS

Developing Standards in History for Students in Grades K-4

Significance of History for the Educated Citizen

Setting standards for history in the schools requires a clear vision of the place and importance of history in the general education of all students. The widespread and growing support for more and better history in the schools, beginning in the early grades of elementary education, is one of the encouraging signs of this decade. The reasons are many, but none more important to a democratic society than this: *knowledge of history is the precondition of political intelligence.* Without history, a society shares no common memory of where it has been, of what its core values are, or of what decisions of the past account for present circumstances. Without history, one cannot undertake any sensible inquiry into the political, social, or moral issues in society. And without historical knowledge and the inquiry it supports, one cannot move to the informed, discriminating citizenship essential to effective participation in the democratic processes of governance and the fulfillment for all our citizens of the nation's democratic ideals.

Today's students, more than ever before, need also a comprehensive understanding of the history of the world, and of the peoples of many cultures and civilizations who have developed ideas, institutions, and ways of life different from students' own. From a balanced and inclusive world history students may gain an appreciation both of the world's many cultures and of their shared humanity and common problems. Students may acquire the habit of seeing matters through others' eyes and come to realize that by studying others, they can also better understand themselves. Historical understanding based on such comparative studies in world history does not require approval or forgiveness for the tragedies either of one's own society or of others; nor does it negate the importance of critically examining alternative value systems and their effects in supporting or denying the basic human rights and aspirations of all peoples. Especially important, an understanding of the history of the world's many cultures can contribute to fostering the kind of mutual patience, respect, and civic courage required in our increasingly pluralistic society and our increasingly interdependent world.

These learnings directly contribute to the education of the *public citizen*, but they uniquely contribute to nurturing the *private individual* as well. Historical memory is the key to self-identity, to seeing one's place in the stream of time, and one's connectedness with all of humankind. We are part of an ancient chain, and the long hand of the past is upon us — for good and for ill — just as our hands will rest on our descendants for years to come. Denied knowledge of one's roots and of one's place in the great stream of human history, the individual is deprived of the fullest sense of self and of shared community on which one's fullest personal development as well as responsible citizenship depends. For these purposes, history and the humanities must occupy an indispensable role in the school curriculum, beginning in the earliest years of the school curriculum.

The Case for History in Grades K-4

For young children, history — along with literature and the arts — provides one of the most enriching studies in which they can be engaged. "What children of this age need," Bruno Bettelheim has written, "is rich food for their imagination, a sense of history, how the present situation came about." History enlarges children's experience, providing, in the words of Philip Phenix, "a sense of personal involvement in exemplary lives and significant events, an appreciation of values and a vision of greatness." History connects each child with his or her roots and develops a sense of personal belonging in the great sweep of human experience.

Fortunately, the nation's educators are increasingly recognizing the importance of history in these early years of schooling, and of the interests and capabilities history fosters in young children. If students are to enjoy these immediate benefits of historical studies which Bettelheim, Phenix, and others have observed, and to lay the foundations on which their continuing development of the major goals addressed above depend, then schools must broaden the curriculum to include historical studies from the earliest school years onward.

Definition of Standards

Standards in history make explicit the goals that all students should have opportunity to acquire, if the purposes just considered are to be achieved. In history, standards are of two types:

1. *Historical thinking skills* that enable children to differentiate past, present, and future time; raise questions; seek and evaluate evidence; compare and analyze historical stories, illustrations, and records from the past; interpret the historical record; and construct historical narratives of their own.

2. *Historical understandings* that define what students should *know* about the history of families, their communities, states, nation, and world. These understandings are drawn from the record of human aspirations, strivings, accomplishments, and failures in at least five spheres of human activity: the social, political, scientific/technological, economic, and cultural (the philosophical/religious/aesthetic), as appropriate for children.

Historical thinking and understanding do not, of course, develop independently of one another. Higher levels of historical thinking depend upon and are linked to the attainment of higher levels of historical understanding. For these reasons, the standards presented in Chapter 3 of this volume provide an integration of historical thinking and understanding.

Basic Principles Guiding the Development of Standards for K-4

History Standards for elementary school children, grades K-4, have been developed with the following principles in mind:

1. Children can, from the earliest elementary grades, begin to build historical understandings and perspectives and to think historically. An important responsibility of schooling in these years is to support the conditions which foster children's natural curiosity and imagination, to provide them opportunities to reach out in time and space, and to expand their world of understanding far beyond the "here and now."

2. Although young children are only in the early stages of acquiring concepts of chronology and time, they easily learn to differentiate time present, time past, and time "long, long ago" — skills on which good programs in historical thinking can then build over grades K-4.

3. To bring history alive, an important part of children's historical studies should be centered in people — the history of families and of people, ordinary and extraordinary, who have lived in children's own community, state, nation, and the world.

4. History becomes especially accessible and interesting to children when approached through stories, myths, legends, and biographies that capture children's imaginations and immerse them in times and cultures of the recent and long-ago past.

5. In addition to stories, children should be introduced to a wide variety of historical artifacts, illustrations, and records that open to them first-hand glimpses into the lives of people in the past: family photos; letters, diaries, and other accounts of the past obtained from family records, local newspapers, libraries, and museums; field trips to historical sites in their neighborhood and community; and visits to "living museums" where actors reenact life long ago.

6. All these resources should be used imaginatively to help children formulate questions for study and to support historical thinking, such as the ability to marshal information; create sound hypotheses; locate events in time and place; compare and contrast past and present; explain historical causes and consequences; analyze historical fiction and illustrations for their accuracy and perspectives, and compare with primary sources that accurately portray life, attitudes, and values in the past; compare different stories about an era or event in the past and the interpretations or perspectives of each; and create historical narratives of their own in the form of stories, letters such as a child long ago might have written, and descriptive accounts of events.

Developing Standards in History for Grades K-4

Topical Organization

Determining the organization by which standards for grades K-4 would be presented involved something of a dilemma, given the variety of curriculum approaches teachers can adopt in developing engaging historical studies for children. In addressing this problem in 1988, the Bradley Commission on History in Schools identified three curricular options for grades K-4:

(1) **A "here — there — then" approach:** This approach first centers instruction in each of these grades in the child's immediate present and then each year reaches out in space and back in time to enlarge children's breadth of geographic and historical understandings to distant places and times long ago. From kindergarten onward, this model introduces children to peoples and cultures throughout the world, and to historical times as distant as the earliest human memories, contained in myths, legends, and heroic tales, which are part of the cultural heritage of the world.

(2) **A modification of the "expanding environments" approach to social studies:** This approach includes, each year, rich studies in history and literature that connect with grade 1 studies of the family, grade 2 studies of the neighborhood, grade 3 studies of the community, and grade 4 studies of the state, but that expand and deepen these studies far beyond their traditional emphasis on the "here and now." Thus, this modified model compares family, community, and state today with family life long ago, and with the people and events of earlier times in the historical development of their community and state. Fully expanded, this model also compares family and community life in the United States with life in the many cultures from which our increasingly diverse population has come, and with the historical experiences and traditions that are part of those cultures.

(3) **A "literature-centered" approach:** This approach focuses instruction each year on compelling selections of literature appropriate for children from many historical periods, and then expands those studies to explore more deeply the historical times they bring to life. This pattern is, essentially, a child's version of the humanities-centered "Great Books" approach to curriculum-making, with literature used to take children into adventurous and deeply engaging excursions through a variety of historical eras and cultures.

In developing standards for history in grades K-4, the Curriculum Task Force sought an organizational structure flexible enough to support improved programs in history under any of these curriculum approaches, rather than assuming a single national curriculum for the schools. The topics believed to meet this need and under which the eight standards in history have been organized are as follows:

Topic 1: Living and Working Together in Families and Communities, Now and Long Ago

Topic 2: The History of Students' Own State or Region

Topic 3: The History of the United States: Its Democratic Principles and Values and the Peoples from Many Cultures Who Have Contributed to Its Cultural, Economic, and Political Heritage

Topic 4: The History of Peoples of Many Cultures around the World

Although organized geographically from "near to far," these topics reach far beyond the traditional content of the "expanding environments" curriculum model for grades K-4 by including at all grade levels studies of the nation and the world, and of the ancient as well as more recent past. How teachers draw upon these standards and how they sequence their programs of instruction should be determined by the particular curriculum approach they have adopted. For example:

(1) **Teachers adopting the "here — there — then" model of curriculum-making** will find standards that connect the child's present world with the long-ago past and with distant cultures at every grade level, K-2 as well as 3-4. Thus, teachers of grades K-2 are not limited to comparative studies of family and community life (Topic 1). They may also select standards from Topics 2-4 that deepen young children's understanding of people, ordinary and extraordinary, who have contributed to the betterment of others' lives in their state, nation, and the world at various times in history; and they can engage children in analyses of compelling stories of individual heroism and epic events from ancient times until today by adopting standards from Topics 2-4, as well.

(2) **Teachers adopting the modified "expanding environments" approach** will find Topics 1 and 2 easily incorporated in their present curriculum and find in Topics 3 and 4 rich opportunities for expanding children's understandings beyond the immediate "here and now."

(3) **Teachers adopting the "literature-centered" approach to history** will find throughout the standards rich inclusions of literature and of associated historical studies of the era or context in which the literary selections were developed. Visiting museums and "living history" sites to observe the clothing, houses, furnishings, tools, and other artifacts referenced in a particular selection of historical fiction or biography; observing the geographic site in which historic events in the story occurred; comparing the characters and descriptions in the story and its illustrations with diaries, documents, photos, and other records of the time to judge the historical authenticity of the work; placing events in their chronological and geographic place on time lines and maps; reenacting episodes in the story through dramatizations; and writing their own narrative accounts are all examples of student achievement of standards on which teachers choosing a literature-centered approach to history can draw.

The standards, in short, define outcomes of instruction. They assume no one curriculum design. Teachers must be free to enter these standards and use them appropriately to meet the interests and instructional needs of the students they are teaching.

Historical Understanding for Grades K-4

History for grades K-4 is a broadly integrative field, recounting and analyzing human aspirations and strivings in at least five spheres of human activity: social, scientific/technological, economic, political, and cultural (the religious/philosophical/aesthetic). Introducing young children to history — the history of families, their communities, their state, nation, and various cultures of the world — at once engages them in the lives, aspirations, struggles, accomplishments, and failures of real people, in all these aspects of their lives.

▶ Through history, children come to deeper understandings of society: of different and changing patterns of family structures, of men's and women's roles, of childhood and of children's roles, of various groups in society, and of relationships among all these individuals and groups.

▶ Through history, children come to deeper understandings of the scientific quest to understand the world we live in and the quest to do better, or more efficiently, everything from producing food to caring for the ill, to transporting goods, to advancing economic security and the well-being of the group. Understandings of the work people have done, the exchange relationships they have developed with others, and the scientific/technological developments that have propelled change are all central to the study of history and of great interest to children.

▶ Through history, children come to a beginning understanding of the political sphere of activity as it has developed in their local community, their state, and their nation. Particularly important are understandings of the core principles and values of American democracy that unite us as a people; of the people and events that have exemplified these principles in local, state, and national history; and of the struggles to bring the rights guaranteed by these principles to all Americans.

▶ Ideas, beliefs, and values have profoundly influenced human actions throughout history. Religion, philosophy, art, and popular culture have all been central to the aspirations and achievements of all societies, and have been a mainspring of historical change from earliest times. Children's explorations of this sphere of human activity, through delving into the literature, sacred writings and oral traditions, drama, art, architecture, music, and dance of a people, bring history to life for children, foster empathy, and deepen their understandings of the human experience.

Historical Thinking

History, properly developed for children in the early years of schooling, can open important opportunities to analyze and develop appreciation for all these spheres of human activity and of the interactions among them. To do so requires that children be engaged in *active* questioning and learning, and not in the passive absorption of facts, names, and dates. Real historical understanding requires that students engage in historical reasoning; listen to and read historical stories, narratives, and literature with meaning; think through cause-effect relationships; interview "old-timers" in their communities; analyze documents, photos, historical newspapers, and the records of the past available in libraries, local museums and historical sites; and construct time lines and historical narratives of their own. Essential to developing historical insights and lasting learning, these skills are also the processes of *active* learning.

Tailored to the capabilities of young students, these activities are capable of developing skills in the following five types of historical thinking:

▶ **Chronological thinking**, developing a beginning sense of historical time — past, present, and future — in order to identify the temporal sequence in which events occurred, measure calendar time, interpret and create time lines, and explain patterns of historical continuity and change.

▶ **Historical comprehension**, including the ability to listen to and read historical stories and narratives with understanding, to identify the basic elements of the narrative or story structure (the characters, situation, sequence of events, their causes, and their outcome); and to develop the ability to describe the past through the eyes and experiences of those who were there, as revealed through their literature, art, artifacts, and other records of their time.

▶ **Historical analysis and interpretation**, including the ability to compare and contrast different experiences, beliefs, motives, traditions, hopes, and fears of people from various groups and backgrounds, and at various times in the past and present; to analyze how these differing motives, interests, beliefs, hopes, and fears influenced people's behaviors; to compare the different perspectives included in different stories about historical people and events; to compare historical fiction and documentary sources about a particular era or event; and to analyze the historical accuracy of fictional accounts.

▶ **Historical research capabilities,** including the ability to formulate historical questions from encounters with historical documents, artifacts, photos, visits to historical sites, and eyewitness accounts; to acquire information concerning the historical time and place where the artifact, document, or other record was created; and to construct a historical narrative or story concerning it.

▶ **Historical issues-analysis and decision-making,** including the ability to identify problems that confronted people in historical literature, the local community, and the state; to analyze the various interests and points of view of people caught up in these situations; to evaluate alternative proposals for dealing with the problem(s); and to analyze whether the decisions reached or the actions taken were good ones and why.

Integrating Historical Thinking and Historical Understandings in Standards for Grades K-4

Chapter 2 presents the K-4 Standards in Historical Thinking, largely independent of historical content in order to specify the quality of thinking desired for each. None of these skills in historical thinking, however, can be developed or even expressed in a vacuum. Every one of them requires historical content in order to function — a relationship clarified in Chapter 3, in which the standards integrating historical understandings and thinking are presented for all four topics in history for grades K-4.

Figure 1 illustrates the approach taken to integrate historical thinking and understandings in the standards. The example is drawn from Topic 2, *The History of Students' Own State or Region.* As illustrated, the five skills in historical thinking (the left side of the diagram) and the three historical understandings students should acquire concerning the history of their state (the right side of the diagram) are integrated in the central area of overlap in the diagram in order to define (immediately below) Standard 3B: What students should be able to do to demonstrate their understanding of the first European, African, and/or Asian/Pacific explorers and settlers in their state or region.

Pages 10 and 11 provide a further illustration of this same standard, presented this time in the format in which the standards are stated (Chapter 3). The selection is again drawn from Topic 2, *The History of Students' Own State or Region.* As illustrated, the standard first presents a statement defining what students should understand: "The history of the first European, African, and/or Asian/Pacific explorers and settlers who came into their state or region."

The standard next presents five statements in a shaded box to specify what students should be able to do to demonstrate their understanding of these early explorers and settlers. Each statement illustrates the integration of historical thinking and historical understandings by marrying a particular thinking skill (e.g., constructing a historical narrative) to a specific historical understanding (e.g., daily life in early settlements of their state or region). The particular thinking skill is further emphasized in the bracketed words following the statement (e.g., **Obtain needed historical data**).

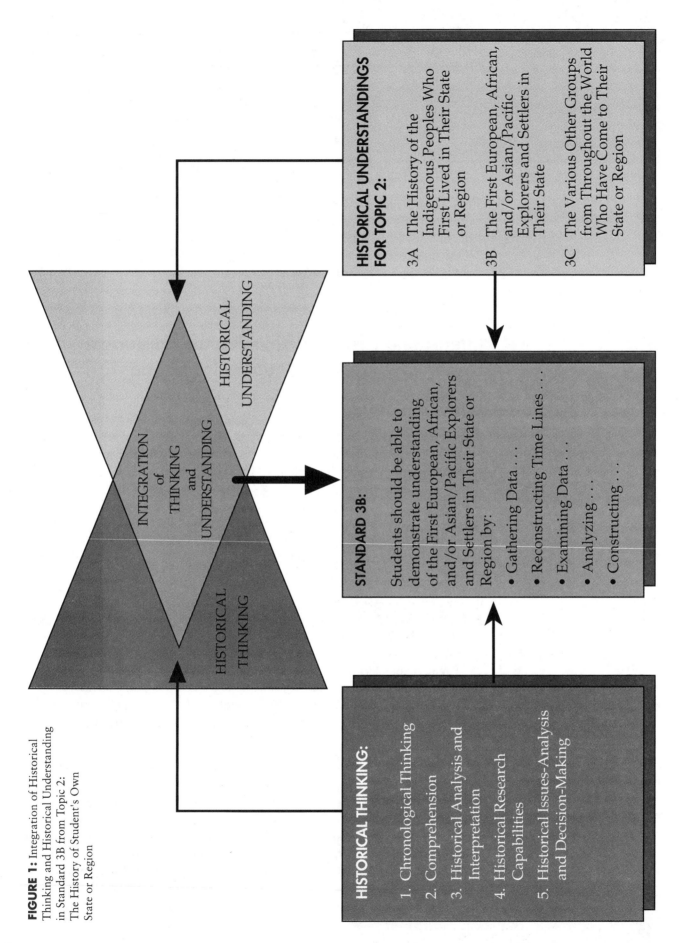

FIGURE 1: Integration of Historical Thinking and Historical Understanding in Standard 3B from Topic 2: The History of Student's Own State or Region

HISTORICAL UNDERSTANDINGS FOR TOPIC 2:

3A The History of the Indigenous Peoples Who First Lived in Their State or Region

3B The First European, African, and/or Asian/Pacific Explorers and Settlers in Their State

3C The Various Other Groups from Throughout the World Who Have Come to Their State or Region

HISTORICAL UNDERSTANDING

INTEGRATION of THINKING and UNDERSTANDING

HISTORICAL THINKING

STANDARD 3B:

Students should be able to demonstrate understanding of the First European, African, and/or Asian/Pacific Explorers and Settlers in Their State or Region by:

- Gathering Data . . . .
- Reconstructing Time Lines . . . .
- Examining Data . . . .
- Analyzing . . . .
- Constructing . . . .

HISTORICAL THINKING:

1. Chronological Thinking
2. Comprehension
3. Historical Analysis and Interpretation
4. Historical Research Capabilities
5. Historical Issues-Analysis and Decision-Making

The particular thinking skill is not the only one that can be employed but is a particularly apt one. Finally, each component of Standard 3B is coded to indicate in which grades the standard can appropriately be developed.

> K-4 indicates the standard is appropriate for grades K-2, as well as for grades 3-4

> 3-4 indicates the standard is appropriate for grades 3-4

Finally, the shaded box is supplemented with examples of student achievement of Standard 3B appropriate for grades K-2 and 3-4.

Questions Concerning These Standards

Q: **Do these Standards require that Topic 2, The History of Students' Own State or Region, be taught at all grades, K-2 and 3-4?**

A: **No.** The local school curriculum and the approach it takes to history for young children will determine when the standards included in Topic 2 are taught, whether partially in grades K-3, exclusively in grade 4, or in some other curriculum arrangement. Once that curriculum decision is made, teachers can enter these standards to determine which ones are appropriate for their students.

Q: **Are teachers of grades 3-4 expected to teach all the standards coded K-4 in the shaded boxes?**

A: **No.** These standards assume that teachers at all grades of early schooling, K-4, will include history in their programs. In that case, standards coded as appropriate for grades K-4 will probably have been studied to some degree during grades K-2, and emphasis can be turned in grades 3 and 4 to those standards that are coded 3-4 and that are better reserved for these later years. Again, these are matters of well-designed, articulated curriculum planning within the jurisdiction of local schools.

Q: **Does the thinking skill incorporated in a particular standard limit teachers to that one skill?**

A: **No.** Each standard highlights a particularly important thinking skill. However, it is understood that good teaching will incorporate more than a single thinking skill to develop these understandings.

Q: **Does the particular thinking skill identified in the standard limit the instructional approaches teachers might use to develop these outcomes with students?**

A: **No.** To take one example, the first bulleted component of Standard 3B, "Gathering data in order to analyze geographic, economic, and religious reasons that brought the first explorers and settlers to their state or region," can be developed through a variety of teaching approaches. Illustrated in the Examples of Student Achievement of Standard 3B presented on pages 10 and 11, these approaches include reading biographies and historical fiction, visiting historic sites and living history museums, and studying historical maps, journals, and other primary sources in order to gather data; engaging in such activities as creating group stories and historical narratives of their own; and creating maps, dramatizations, and "shoebox picture strips" to depict and explain the reasons people came and the experiences they encountered.

TOPIC 2

The History of Students' Own State or Region

Statements of the historical understandings that students should acquire

STANDARD 3

Students Should Understand: *The people, events, problems, and ideas that were significant in creating the history of their state.*

Students Should Be Able to:

3A Demonstrate understanding of the history of indigenous peoples who first lived in their state or region by:

[K-4] Drawing upon data in paintings and artifacts to hypothesize about the culture of the early Hawaiians or Native Americans who are known to have lived in the state or region, e.g., the Anasazi of the Southwest, the Makah of the Northwest coast, the Eskimos/Inupiat of Alaska, the Creeks of the Southeast, the Mississippians (Cahokia), or the Mound Builders. [**Formulate historical questions**]

[K-4] Drawing upon legends and myths of the Native Americans or Hawaiians who lived in students' state or region in order to describe personal accounts of their history. [**Read historical narratives imaginatively**]

[3-4] Comparing and contrasting how Native American or Hawaiian life today differs from the life of these same groups over 100 years ago. [**Compare and contrast differing sets of ideas**]

Grades K-2

Examples of student achievement of Standard 3A include:

♦ Draw upon myths and legends such as *Arrow to the Sun* by Gerald McDermott, *How Man Slowed the Sun* by Suelyn Ching Tune, *Her Seven Brothers, Alaskan Igloo Tales* by Edward L. Keithahn, *Grandmother Stories: Indian Tales of the Northwest* by Nashone, *It Is Still That Way* by Bryd Baylor, and *How the Stars Fell into the Sky, A Navajo Legend* by Jerrie Oughton, in order to make a class picture of the origins and culture of the Native Americans or Hawaiians in the state.

♦ Examine artifacts found at museums, historical sites, or in pictures to generate questions and to hypothesize about early Hawaiian or Native American culture such as: *Who made this object? Why was it made? What could it have been used for? How was it made? What do the materials tell you about the environment?*

40

TOPIC 2: THE HISTORY OF STUDENTS' OWN STATE OR REGION

Grades 3-4

Examples of student achievement of Standard 3A include:

▶ Draw upon myths, legends, archaeological evidence, visits to historic sites, such as Angel Mounds State Historic Site (in southwestern Indiana), and pictures of artifacts to develop historical narratives about the origin and culture of the earliest inhabitants of the region or state.

▶ Draw upon books such as *Dogsong* by G. Paulson to compare the life and culture of Native Americans long ago and today.

Students Should Be Able to:

3B. Demonstrate understanding of the history of the first European, African, and/or Asian-Pacific explorers and settlers who came to their state or region by:

`3-4` Gathering data in order to analyze geographic, economic, and religious reasons that brought the first explorers and settlers to the state or region. [Obtain needed historical data]

`3-4` Reconstructing in time lines the order of early explorations and settlements including explorers, early settlements, and cities. [Establish temporal order]

`K-4` Examining visual data in order to describe ways in which early settlers adapted to, utilized, and changed the environment. [Draw upon visual data]

`3-4` Analyzing some of the interactions that occurred between the Native Americans or Hawaiians and the first European, African, and Asian-Pacific explorers and settlers in the students' state or region. [Read historical narratives imaginatively]

`K-4` Using a variety of sources to construct a historical narrative about daily life in the early settlements of their state or region. [Obtain needed historical data]

Statement identifying the second understanding of Standard 3: the first European, African, and Asian-Pacific explorers and settlers

*Components of Standard 3B, demonstrating integration of historical understanding and **thinking***

Grades K-2

Examples of student achievement of Standard 3B include:

▶ Draw upon biographies of early explorers and books such as *Sarah Morton's Day* by Kate Waters, *Going West* by Jean Van Leuwen, and *On the Day Peter Stuyvesant Sailed into Town* by Arnold Lobel, in order to describe, either orally or visually, the life of early explorers and settlers.

▶ After visiting "living history" and other local museums, historic sites, and libraries, visually depict or develop a group story about daily life in early state history. (Encourage students to share information gained from family "field trips.")

Examples of student achievement of Standard 3B

Grades 3-4

Examples of student achievement of Standard 3B include:

▶ Make a picture map illustrating the people, places, and events of such early explorations of their state or region as those of Spanish explorers, French and English fur traders, Lewis and Clark, Marquette and Joliet, and James Beckwourth.

▶ Construct a historical map of the state or region locating early forts, missions, settlements, and cities.

41

Three Policy Issues

Ensuring Equity for All Students

The purposes of the national standards developed in this document are three-fold: (1) to establish high expectations for what all students should know and be able to do; (2) to clarify what constitutes successful achievement; and (3) *most significantly, to promote equity in the learning opportunities and resources to be provided all students in the nation's schools.*

Standards in and of themselves cannot ensure remediation of the pervasive inequalities in the educational opportunities currently available to students. The roots of these problems are deep and widely manifested in gross inequities in school financing, in resource allocations, and in practices of discriminatory "lower tracks" and "dumbed down" curricula that continue to deny large sectors of the nation's children equal educational opportunity.

What the national commitment to high achievement standards for all students *can* do is to serve as an engine of change: (1) defining for all students the goals essential to success in a rapidly changing global economy and in a society undergoing wrenching social, technological, and economic change; and (2) establishing the moral obligation to provide equity in the educational resources required to help all students attain these goals.

As for resources, if students are to achieve the understandings and thinking skills specified in these Standards, they must have equal access to well-prepared history teachers and to engaging, balanced, accurate, and challenging curricular materials. For these reasons the success of Goals 2000 and of the systemic educational reform program it has launched requires the provision of high quality professional development in history and in pedagogy for teachers who are not prepared to teach the content or thinking skills presented in this document. Equally important, all students must be provided with the best available curricular materials needed to support these standards.

As Robert Hutchins said many years ago: "The best education for the best should be the best education for all." Every child is entitled to and must have equal access to excellence in the goals their teachers strive to help them achieve and in the instructional resources and opportunities required to reach those ends. Nothing less is acceptable in a democratic society; no commitment is more essential to meeting the challenges — economic, social, and ethical — confronting this nation in the years ahead.

Providing Adequate Instructional Time for History

One of the major commitments called for in Goals 2000 and in the reform movement supported by this legislation is the need to allocate considerably more time in the school day to the core academic subjects, history among them. The "drill the skills" and "minimum competencies" approaches of the 1970s virtually extinguished content studies in elementary schools, with the result that not only did content languish, so too did the higher-order thinking and reading skills that are dependent upon rich subject-matter content, if students are to have something to "think about."

The schools today are in the process of remediating those lacks and the high costs they exacted in students' intellectual development. In doing so, it is especially important that schools provide adequate time for history in all grades, K-4. Linking these historical studies to related studies in geography, civics, literature, and the arts is one important way to do so, and is considered below.

Linking History to Related Studies in Geography, Civics, Literature, and the Arts in an Integrated or Interdisciplinary Curriculum for Grades K-4

Two factors encourage linking history to related studies in the social studies, literature, and the arts in grades K-4:

(1) **History itself is a highly integrative field,** engaging children in studies not only of the people and events in the history of their community, state, nation, and world, but opening as well the study of the geographic places in which these events occurred; the ideas, beliefs, and values that influenced how people acted in their daily lives; the rules, laws, and institutions they established and lived by; the oral traditions and literature, music, art, architecture, and dance they created; and the technological and scientific developments they invented, or adopted, in their quest to improve daily life. In short, studies in history necessarily include geographic, economic, political, social, and scientific studies, as well as studies in the arts.

(2) **Teachers of grades K-4 normally are responsible for the entire curriculum and therefore are uniquely able to schedule activities that cut across subject lines and develop standards from two or more fields in a single lesson.** Thus, lessons in literature can include literary selections from historical fiction, biography, and other readings important to the history curriculum as well as to the language arts. In turn, activities in creating group stories in history (K-1) and individual historical narratives, letters, journals, and so on (grades 2-4) in children's studies of history are important in furthering standards in English as well as in history. So, too, can lessons simultaneously develop certain standards in history and in civics, in geography, in economics, in the arts, and — to some degree — in mathematics and science.

Developing the interdisciplinary or integrated curriculum is not without pitfalls. Teachers should be aware of some of the problems that led to the widespread withdrawal from these approaches in the curriculum reform movement of the 1960s. One safeguard is to keep clearly in mind the unique characteristics of each field, and to respect those characteristics in any curriculum plan that seeks to capitalize upon the natural affinities among these fields. The National Standards being separately developed in these various fields as well as in history provide an important contribution to that end.

Photograph by Bert Seal
San Diego County Office of Education

Students, Baltimore City Schools

Photograph by Bert Seal
San Diego County Office of Education

Standards in Historical Thinking

Children's study of history involves much more than the passive absorption of facts, names, dates, and places. Real historical understanding requires students to engage in historical thinking: to raise questions and to marshal evidence in support of their answers; to read historical narratives and fiction; to consult historical documents, journals, diaries, artifacts, historic sites, and other records from the past; and to do so imaginatively — taking into account the time and places in which these records were created and comparing the multiple points of view of those on the scene at the time.

Real historical understanding also requires that children have opportunities to create historical narratives of their own. Such narratives may take many forms: group stories dictated to the teacher in grades K-1, and individual stories, letters such as a child of the time may have written, journals, and reports in grades 2-4, for example.

Historical understanding also requires that students thoughtfully listen to and read the historical narratives created by others. Well written historical narratives are interpretative, revealing conditions, changes, and consequences, and explaining why things happened as they did. Following such narratives, and analyzing the events they describe and the explanations they offer, promote important skills in historical thinking.

Because of the importance of historical fiction in opening the past to children and engaging their interests in the people and events of long ago, it is especially important for children to learn to analyze these stories for their historical accuracy, to compare these stories and their illustrations with primary sources — historical artifacts, photos, diaries, and other records of the past — and to differentiate fact and fiction. Children should also have opportunities to compare different stories about a historical figure or event in order to analyze the facts each author includes or omits, and the interpretations or point of view communicated by each — important early steps in the development of students' abilities to compare competing historical interpretations of events.

Students engaged in activities of the kinds just considered will draw upon skills in the following five types of historical thinking:

1. Chronological Thinking
2. Historical Comprehension
3. Historical Analysis and Interpretation
4. Historical Research Capabilities
5. Historical Issues-Analysis and Decision-Making

These skills, while presented in five separate categories, are nonetheless interactive and mutually supportive. In conducting historical research or creating a historical story of their own, for example, students must be able to draw upon skills in all five categories. Beyond the skills of conducting their research, students must, for example, be able to comprehend historical artifacts and records consulted in their search, analyze their purpose and importance, and demonstrate a grasp of the historical time (e.g., long, long ago) and geographic place in which the problem or events developed.

In short, these five sets of skills, developed in the following pages as the five Standards in Historical Thinking, are statements of the **outcomes** we desire students to achieve. They are not mutually exclusive when put into practice, nor do they prescribe a particular teaching sequence to be followed. Teachers will draw upon all these Thinking Standards, as appropriate, to develop their teaching plans and to guide students through challenging programs of study in history.

Finally, it is important to point out that these five sets of Standards in Historical Thinking are defined in the following pages largely independent of historical content in order to specify the quality of thinking desired for each. It is essential to understand, however, that these skills do not develop, nor can they be practiced, in a vacuum. Every one of these skills requires historical content in order to function — a relationship that is made explicit in Chapter 3, which presents the standards integrating historical understandings and thinking.

Overview of Standards in Historical Thinking

Standard 1. Chronological Thinking

A. Distinguish between past, present, and future time.

B. Identify in historical narratives the temporal structure of a historical narrative or story.

C. Establish temporal order in constructing their [students'] own historical narratives.

D. Measure and calculate calendar time.

E. Interpret data presented in time lines.

F. Create time lines.

G. Explain change and continuity over time.

Standard 2. Historical Comprehension

A. Reconstruct the literal meaning of a historical passage.

B. Identify the central question(s) the historical narrative addresses.

C. Read historical narratives imaginatively.

D. Evidence historical perspectives.

E. Draw upon the data in historical maps.

F. Draw upon visual and mathematical data presented in graphics.

G. Draw upon the visual data presented in photographs, paintings, cartoons, and architectural drawings.

Standard 3. Historical Analysis and Interpretation

A. Formulate questions to focus their inquiry or analysis.

B. Identify the author or source of the historical document or narrative.

C. Compare and contrast differing sets of ideas, values, personalities, behaviors, and institutions.

D. Analyze historical fiction.

E. Distinguish between fact and fiction.

F. Compare different stories about a historical figure, era, or event.

G. Analyze illustrations in historical stories

H. Consider multiple perspectives.

I. Explain causes in analyzing historical actions.

J. Challenge arguments of historical inevitability.

K. Hypothesize influences of the past.

Standard 4. Historical Research Capabilities

A. Formulate historical questions.

B. Obtain historical data.

C. Interrogate historical data.

D. Marshal needed knowledge of the time and place, and construct a story, explanation, or historical narrative.

Standard 5. Historical Issues-Analysis and Decision-Making

A. Identify issues and problems in the past.

B. Compare the interests and values of the various people involved.

C. Suggest alternative choices for addressing the problem.

D. Evaluate alternative courses of action.

E. Prepare a position or course of action on an issue.

F. Evaluate the consequences of a decision.

STANDARD 1

Chronological Thinking

Chronological thinking is at the heart of historical reasoning. Without a clear sense of historical time — time past, present, and future — students are bound to see events as one great tangled mess. Without a strong sense of chronology — of when events occurred and in what temporal order — it is impossible for students to examine relationships among them or to explain historical causality. Chronology provides the mental scaffolding for organizing historical thought.

In developing students' chronological thinking, an important share of instructional time should be given to the use of well constructed *historical narratives*: literary narratives including biographies and historical literature, and well written narrative histories that have the quality of "stories well told." Well crafted narratives such as these have the power to grip and hold students' attention. Thus engaged, the reader (or young listener) is able to focus on what the narrator discloses: the temporal structure of events unfolding over time, the actions and intentions of those who were there, the temporal connections between antecedents and their consequences.

It is these characteristics of well structured historical narratives that probably account for the relationships that have been observed between the use of narratives and young students' developing concepts of time and temporal causation. Responding to well chosen historical narratives, myths, stories, and fables read by the teacher, young children can determine their temporal structure — their "beginning," "middle," and "end" — and retell, reenact, or illustrate the story to put its important developments into correct temporal sequence. They might illustrate, too, the different ending that might have come about, had one of the characters chosen a different course of action — the beginnings of causal and contingency thinking in the elementary years.

Long before young children are ready to calculate calendar time, they are able to use such concepts as "long, long ago," "long ago," "yesterday," "today," and "tomorrow," and to put historical developments they have learned about in correct temporal relationships according to broad categories such as these. Children should also be developing their ability to identify examples of changes and continuity over time.

Children by grade 4 have been observed to use more precise historical eras, such as the "time of empires" or the "American Revolution." By this time, mathematical understandings should be sufficiently developed to support students' meaningful use of years, decades, and centuries to calculate historical time, and to create more elaborate systems of "chronological scaffolding" on which more challenging analyses can be undertaken.

Photograph by Bert Seal
San Diego County Office of Education

Students Should Be Able to:

A. **Distinguish between past, present, and future time.**

B. **Identify the temporal structure of a historical narrative or story:** its beginning, middle, and end (the latter defined as the outcome of a particular beginning).

C. **Establish temporal order in constructing their [students'] own historical narratives:** working *forward* from some beginning through its development, to some end or outcome; working *backward* from some issue, problem, or event to explain its origins and its development over time.

D. **Measure and calculate calendar time** by days, weeks, months, years, decades, centuries.

E. **Interpret data presented in time lines.**

F. **Create time lines** by designating appropriate equidistant intervals of time and recording events according to the temporal order in which they occurred.

G. **Explain change and continuity over time.**

Grades K-2

Examples of student achievement include:

▶ On listening to or reading historical stories, myths, and narratives, reconstruct the basic organization of the narrative — its beginning, middle, and end — and place events in their correct sequence.

▶ In creating historical narratives of their own, such as their family's, their school's, or community's history, establish a chronology for the story, providing a beginning, middle, and end.

▶ Develop "picture time lines" of their own lives or of events in the history of their own or another family, using photos from home, drawing pictures to fill any gaps, and arranging the set chronologically on long sheets of butcher paper, along a "clothes line," or pasted on successive pages of a photo album.

▶ Differentiate broad categories of historical time, such as "long, long ago," "yesterday," "today," and "tomorrow."

▶ Measure calendar time by days, weeks, and months.

▶ Identify examples of change and continuity in their own lives, in the history of their school and community, and in the ways people lived long ago and today.

Grades 3-4

Examples of student achievement include all of the foregoing plus:

▶ Group historical events by broadly defined eras in the history of their local community and state.

▶ Measure calendar time by years, decades, and centuries.

▶ Construct time lines of significant historical developments in their community and state, identifying the dates at which each occurred and placing them sequentially along a date line that marks at evenly spaced intervals the years, decades, and/or centuries appropriate to the time period under investigation.

◗ Interpret data presented in time lines by identifying the time at which events occurred and the sequence in which events developed.

◗ Trace patterns of change and continuity in the history of their community, state, and nation and in the lives of people of various cultures from times long ago until today.

STANDARD 2

Historical Comprehension

One of the defining features of historical narratives is their believable recounting of human events. To read such accounts with understanding, students must learn to recognize the chronological structure through which the narrative develops — its beginning, middle, and end — and to identify such basic elements of the narrative structure as the characters involved, the situation or setting in which the narrative takes place, the sequence of events through which the story unfolds, the initiating or causal event(s) that led to these developments, and the results or consequences of these actions.

Beyond providing a believable recounting of human events, historical narratives also have the power to disclose the intentions of the characters involved, the difficulties they encountered, and, as Jerome Bruner has observed, the "psychological and cultural reality in which the participants in history actually lived." To read historical stories, biographies, autobiographies, and narratives with comprehension, therefore, students must develop the ability to read imaginatively, to take into account what the narrative reveals of the humanity of the individuals involved — their probable motives and intentions, their hopes, doubts, fears, strengths, and weaknesses. Comprehending historical narratives requires, also, that students develop the ability to describe the past on its own terms, through the eyes and experiences of those who were there, as revealed through their literature, diaries, letters, arts, artifacts, and the like; and to avoid "present-mindedness," not judging the past solely in terms of the norms and values of today, but taking into account the historical context in which the event unfolded — the values, outlook, crises, options, and contingencies of that time and place.

Acquiring these skills begins in the early years of childhood through the use of superbly written stories and biographies that capture children's imagination, evoke the ethos and perspectives of the past, and provide an important foundation for students' continuing historical study.

Beyond these important outcomes, students in grades 3 and 4 should also develop the skills needed to comprehend historical narratives that *explain* as well as *recount* the course of events. These skills include: (1) identifying the central question the historical narrative seeks to answer; (2) defining the purpose or point of view from which the narrative has been constructed; (3) following the historical explanation with meaning; and (4) recognizing the cues that signal how the author has organized the text.

Comprehending these historical narratives will also be facilitated if students are able to draw upon the data presented in historical maps, graphics, and a variety of visual sources such as historical photographs, political cartoons, paintings, and architecture in order to clarify, illustrate, or elaborate upon the information presented in the text.

Students Should Be Able to:

A. **Reconstruct the literal meaning of a historical passage** by identifying who was involved, what happened, where it happened, what events led to these developments, and what consequences or outcomes followed.

B. **Identify the central question(s)** the historical narrative addresses and the purpose, perspective, or point of view from which it has been constructed.

C. **Read historical narratives imaginatively,** taking into account (a) the historical context in which the event unfolded — the values, outlook, crises, options, and contingencies of that time and place; and (b) what the narrative reveals of the humanity of the individuals involved — their probable motives, hopes, fears, strengths, and weaknesses.

D. **Evidence historical perspectives** — the ability (a) to describe the past on its own terms, through the eyes and experiences of those who were there, as revealed through their literature, diaries, letters, arts, artifacts, and the like; and (b) to avoid "present-mindedness," judging the past solely in terms of present-day norms and values.

E. **Draw upon data in historical maps** in order to obtain or clarify information on the geographic setting in which the historical event occurred, its relative and absolute location, the distances and directions involved, the natural and man-made features of the place, and critical relationships in the spatial distributions of those features and historical event occurring there.

F. **Draw upon the visual and mathematical data presented in graphics,** including charts, tables, pie and bar graphs, flow charts, Venn diagrams, and other graphic organizers to clarify, illustrate, or elaborate upon information presented in the historical narrative.

G. **Draw upon the visual data presented in photographs, paintings, cartoons, and architectural drawings** in order to clarify, illustrate, or elaborate upon information presented in the historical narrative.

Grades K-2

Examples of student achievement include:

▶ On listening to or reading historical stories, myths, legends, and narratives, reconstruct the literal meaning of the passage by correctly recounting who was involved; the events that occurred; where they happened; what motives, disclosed in the passage, led to these developments; and the consequences or outcomes that followed.

▶ Listen to or read historical stories, myths, legends, and narratives imaginatively by developing warranted suggestions of the probable motives, hopes, fears, strengths, and weaknesses of the individuals involved.

▶ Read geographic symbols and identify the geographic features of places represented in picture maps, air photos, and terrain models of places now and in the past.

▶ Read and interpret the visual data presented in historical photographs, paintings, and drawings of the people, places, and historical events under study.

Grades 3-4

Examples of student achievement include all of the foregoing plus:

▶ Put themselves "in the shoes" of those who were there by describing the past as people of that time reported seeing or experiencing it.

◗ Read geographic symbols, map scales, and directional indicators in order to obtain such information from historical maps as: the geographic features of the setting in which events occurred, their absolute and relative locations, and the distances and directions involved.

◗ Read and interpret the visual and mathematical data presented in simple flow charts, pie graphs, and Venn diagrams.

STANDARD 3

Historical Analysis and Interpretation

One of the important tasks teachers face in helping children become critical, analytical thinkers as well as thoughtful readers of historical narratives is fostering their intellectual independence and overcoming tendencies to look to teachers for cues, to seek the one "right answer," and to accept without question the printed word as authoritative and true. Young children come to school curious, filled with imagination, eager to reach out, discover, and learn, unless home or prior school experiences have thwarted their development of these natural powers in early childhood. The good teacher of young children will work to create the classroom climate and learning opportunities rich in inviting materials that capture children's interest, fuel their imagination, and pose issues and problems for thinking and resolution.

Teachers will find in history many resources to foster these ends: lively, compelling stories and biographies that catch children up in the real problems, issues, and dilemmas encountered by people at various times in history, and that disclose the variety of perspectives, feelings, motivations, and responses of different peoples involved in the situation; field trips and visits to historic sites and museums; and a rich variety of historical documents, photos, artifacts, and other records of the past that present alternative voices and accounts of events, and that confront students with more than one interpretation of the past.

Many of these resources will be found in local libraries and in the historical collections or files of local newspapers, local museums, and in the collections or personal experiences of parents, and other people in the community. Teachers should cultivate the professional ties and support librarians are eager to offer them, and not hesitate to ask the assistance of historians and geographers in a local college, many of whom are pleased to assist.

In such a classroom setting, children as young as kindergartners can become enthusiastically involved in real historical issues and events, engage actively in examining such data, and analyze and interpret the data for themselves. As has often been noted, thinking cannot occur in a vacuum. Classrooms rich in the historical resources proposed here support even the youngest children with compelling opportunities for active thinking.

Among the analytic thinking skills children should be developing through inviting experiences such as these are the ability to examine a situation and raise questions or define problems for themselves; compare differing ideas, interests, perspectives, actions, and institutions represented in these sources; and elaborate upon what they read and see to develop interpretations, explanations, or solutions to the questions they have raised and the evidence before them.

Students Should Be Able to:

A. **Formulate questions to focus their inquiry and analysis.**

B. **Identify the author or source of the historical document or narrative and assess its credibility.**

C. **Compare and contrast differing sets of ideas,** values, personalities, behaviors, and institutions by identifying likenesses and differences.

D. **Analyze historical fiction** on such criteria as the accuracy of the story's historical details and sequence of events; and the point of view or interpretation presented by the author through the words, actions, and descriptions of the characters and events in the story.

E. **Distinguish fact and fiction** by comparing documentary sources on historical figures and events with the fictional characters and events included in the story and its illustrations.

F. **Compare different stories about a historical figure, era, or event** and analyze the different portrayals or perspectives they present.

G. **Analyze illustrations in historical stories** for the information they reveal and compare with historic sites, museum artifacts, historical photos, and other documents to judge their accuracy.

H. **Consider multiple perspectives** in the records of human experience by demonstrating how their differing motives, beliefs, interests, hopes, and fears influenced individual and group behaviors.

I. **Explain causes in analyzing historical actions,** including (a) the importance of the individual in history, of human will, intellect, and character; (b) the influence of ideas, human interests, and beliefs; and (c) the role of chance, the accidental, and the irrational.

J. **Challenge arguments of historical inevitability** by giving examples of how different choices could have led to different consequences.

K. **Hypothesize the influences of the past,** including both the limitations and opportunities made possible by past decisions.

Grades K-2

Examples of student achievement include:

- Formulate questions to direct their investigation and analysis of family artifacts, historical documents, sites, and other records of the past.

- In listening to or reading historical stories, myths, legends, and narratives, compare and contrast the different experiences of people in the narrative and their possible motives, beliefs, and reactions in the situation.

- In listening to or reading historical narratives, myths, legends, and stories, identify the differing motives, beliefs, interests, hopes, and fears of different people caught up in the event, and analyze how those feelings influenced their behaviors.

- In studying family and community life, compare and contrast likenesses and differences between people's lives, activities, beliefs, traditions, family structures, institutions, and so on at various times in the past and present, and among various groups with differing ethnic, religious, and national backgrounds.

- Suggest how things might have turned out differently if a character in a historical story, legend, myth, or narrative had acted differently.

Grades 3-4

Examples of student achievement include all of the foregoing plus:

▶ Identify the author's main points and the purpose or point of view from which the narrative has been written.

▶ Distinguish between historical facts presented in historical documents and narratives, and the generalizations or interpretations an author draws concerning those facts.

▶ Suggest how things might have turned out differently if those involved in a historical event in their state or nation's history had chosen a different course of action.

▶ Analyze historical narratives to identify the facts the author has provided and to evaluate the credibility of the generalization or interpretation the author has presented.

▶ Compare two or more historical sources and develop a sound interpretation of the issue or event depicted.

▶ Compare historical biographies or stories written about historical events by contrasting the facts included or omitted in each and the point of view of the author(s) of each.

▶ Compare the characters and events described in historical fiction with primary sources such as the historic sites themselves; artifacts of the time available in museums; journals, diaries, and photos of the historical figures in the story; and news articles and other records from the period in order to judge the historical accuracy of the story.

STANDARD 4

Historical Research Capabilities

Perhaps no aspect of historical thinking is as exciting to students or as productive of their growth in historical thinking as "doing history." Such inquiries can be generated by encounters with historical documents, eyewitness accounts, letters, diaries, artifacts, photos, a visit to a historic site, a record of oral history, or other evidence of the past.

Worthy inquiries are especially likely to develop if the documents students encounter are rich with the voices of people caught up in the event and sufficiently diverse to bring alive to students the interests, beliefs, and concerns of peoples with differing backgrounds and opposing viewpoints or perspectives of the events.

Meaningful historical inquiry proceeds with the formulation of a problem or set of questions worth pursuing. In the most direct approach, students might be encouraged to analyze the document, record, or site itself. Who produced it, when, how, and why? What is the evidence of its authenticity, authority, and credibility? What does it tell them of the point of view, background, and interests of its author or creator? What else must they discover in order to construct a story, explanation, or narrative of the event of which this document or artifact is a part?

Obtaining needed background information can send students on a search for additional resources. Providing students access to a school library, history books, interviews with experts in the community, knowledgeable parents and community residents, or other documents will sometimes be required. In this process the teacher, too, can join in the search and share in the process of discovery, thereby communicating to students that historical inquiry is a search in which answers are not known in advance, and that finding and interpreting the results is a genuine process of knowledge-building.

Students Should Be Able to:

A. **Formulate historical questions** from encounters with historical documents, eyewitness accounts, letters, diaries, artifacts, photos, historical sites, art, architecture, and other records from the past.

B. **Obtain historical data** from a variety of sources, including: library and museum collections, historic sites, historical photos, journals, diaries, eyewitness accounts, newspapers, and the like; documentary films; and so on.

C. **Interrogate historical data** by determining by whom and when it was created; testing the data source for its credibility, authority and authenticity; and detecting and evaluating bias, distortion, and propaganda by omission, suppression, or invention of facts.

D. **Marshal needed information of the time and place** in order to construct a story, explanation, or historical narrative.

Grades K-2

Examples of student achievement include:

▶ In obtaining information about family life in the recent and long-ago past, develop questions, conduct interviews, collect family photos and other records from the past, and present their information orally, through illustrations, and through stories.

Grades 3-4

Examples of student achievement include:

▶ In researching the history of their local community and state, formulate questions, obtain information from interviews, field trips, historic records available from local newspapers, libraries, government offices, and museums, and use the information they obtain to create data retrieval charts, displays, and historical narratives describing events in the past.

Student interviewing Grandmother Geddy, a reenactment of a historical person in 18th-century Williamsburg, Virginia Photograph courtesy of the Colonial Williamsburg Foundation

STANDARD 5

Historical Issues-Analysis and Decision-Making

Issue-centered analysis and problem solving activities place students squarely in the center of historical dilemmas with which people have coped at critical moments in the past and near-present. Providing children in grades K-4 opportunity to examine such issues in historical literature and in the history of their local community, state, and nation fosters their personal involvement in these events. If well chosen, these activities promote the development of skills and attitudes essential to citizenship in a democratic society.

Among those skills appropriate for grades K-4 are the ability to analyze a situation; define the issue, problem, or dilemma confronting people in that situation; suggest alternative choices for addressing the problem; evaluate the possible consequences — costs as well as benefits — of each; propose an action; and judge its consequences.

The problems confronting people in well written historical fiction, fables, legends, and myths as well as in historical records of the past are usually value-laden. For this reason, examining these dilemmas, the choices before the people who confronted them, and the consequences of the decisions they made provide opportunities for children to consider the values and beliefs that have influenced human decisions both for good and for ill. They provide opportunities, as well, for students to deepen their understanding and appreciation of such democratic principles and values as individual responsibility, concern for the rights and welfare of others, truth, justice, freedom, and equality of opportunity.

Students Should Be Able to:

A. **Identify problems and dilemmas** confronting people in historical stories, myths, legends, and fables, and in the history of their schools, community, state, nation, and the world.

B. **Analyze the interests, values, and points of view** of those involved in the dilemma or problem situation.

C. **Identify causes of the problem or dilemma.**

D. **Propose alternative ways of resolving the problem or dilemma** and evaluate each in terms of ethical considerations (is it fair? just?), the interests of the different peoples involved, and the likely consequences of each proposal.

E. **Formulate a position or course of action on an issue** by identifying the nature of the problem, analyzing the underlying factors contributing to the problem, and choosing a plausible solution from a choice of carefully evaluated options.

F. **Identify the solution** chosen by characters in the story or in the historical situation; *or*, recommend a course of action themselves.

G. **Evaluate the consequences of the actions taken.**

Grades K-2

Examples of student achievement include:

◗ Examine the problems and dilemmas confronting people in stories and biographies about historical people who "made a difference," and define the problem, the action(s) taken to resolve it, and the consequences or results.

◗ Formulate an alternative course of action that might have been taken, and analyze how things might have turned out differently if that choice had been made.

◗ Identify the interests, values, and points of view of different people caught up in a problem situation portrayed in a fable, myth, legend, or selection of historical fiction, and analyze how their interests and values influenced the choices they made.

◗ Propose a plan of action for solving a problem in their school or local community. *What were some of the causes (e.g., in past decisions) that contributed to the problem? How will their proposed action affect others and contribute to resolving the problem? Does it show concern for the rights and welfare of others? Is it fair and just?*

Grades 3-4

Examples of student achievement include the foregoing plus:

◗ Identify issues and problems in the history of their community and state, the various people involved, and the interests and perspectives of each.

◗ Evaluate the alternative actions that were proposed or might have been offered for resolving the problem, the consequences of the action taken, and compare with the consequences that might have followed had an alternative choice been made.

◗ Apply these same skills to the analysis of a contemporary issue in the students' local community or state which has its roots in past decisions and which requires resolution today.

*Students at Muirlands Middle School
San Diego City Schools, San Diego, CA*

A family observing a reenactment of the work of an 18th century artisan at the Geddy House and Foundry in colonial Williamsburg. Photograph courtesy of the Colonial Williamsburg Foundation

Standards in History for Grades K-4

Overview of the Eight Standards, Organized by Topic

Topic 1: Living and Working Together in Families and Communities, Now and Long Ago

Standard 1: Family Life Now and in the Recent Past; Family Life in Various Places Long Ago

Standard 2: History of Students' Local Community and How Communities in North America Varied Long Ago

Topic 2: The History of the Students' Own State or Region

Standard 3: The People, Events, Problems, and Ideas that Created the History of Their State

Topic 3: The History of the United States: Democratic Principles and Values and the People from Many Cultures Who Contributed to Its Cultural, Economic and Political Thinking

Standard 4: How Democratic Values Came to Be, and How They Have Been Exemplified by People, Events, and Symbols

Standard 5: The Causes and Nature of Various Movements of Large Groups of People into and within the United States, Now and Long Ago

Standard 6: Regional Folklore and Cultural Contributions That Helped to Form Our National Heritage

Topic 4: The History of Peoples of Many Cultures around the World

Standard 7: Selected Attributes and Historical Developments of Various Societies in Africa, the Americas, Asia, and Europe

Standard 8: Major Discoveries in Science and Technology, Their Social and Economic Effects, and the Scientists and Inventors from Many Groups and Regions Responsible for Them

"Laundry on a Snowy Day" an 18th-century woodcut by Suzuki Harunobu Tokyo National Museum

Chinese Dragon Festival
San Diego City Schools
Photograph by David Vigilante

TOPIC 1

Living and Working Together in Families and Communities, Now and Long Ago

STANDARD 1

Students Should Understand: *Family life now and in the recent past; family life in various places long ago.*

Students Should Be Able to:

1A Demonstrate understanding of family life now and in the past by:

K-4 Investigating a family history for at least two generations, identifying various members and their connections in order to construct a time line. *(Teachers should help students understand that families are people from whom they receive love and support. Understanding that many students are raised in non-traditional family structures — i.e., single-parent families, foster homes, guardians raising children — teachers must be sensitive and protect family privacy.)* [**Establish temporal order**]

K-4 From data gathered through family artifacts, photos, and interviews with older relatives and/or other people who play a significant part in a student's life, drawing possible conclusions about roles, jobs, schooling experiences, and other aspects of family life in the recent past. [**Draw upon historical and visual data**]

K-4 For various cultures represented in the classroom, comparing and contrasting family life now with family life over time and between various cultures and considering such things as communication, technology, homes, transportation, recreation, school and cultural traditions. [**Distinguish between past and present**]

K-4 Examining and formulating questions about early records, diaries, family photographs, artifacts, and architectural drawings obtained through a local newspaper or historical society in order to describe family life in their local community or state long ago. [**Formulate historical questions**]

K-4 Comparing and contrasting family life now with family life in the local community or state long ago by considering such things as roles, jobs, communication, technology, style of homes, transportation, schools, religious observances, and cultural traditions. [**Compare and contrast**]

Grades K-2

Examples of student achievement of Standard 1A include:

▶ Present a family history through two generations in a picture time line, family tree, or oral presentation. Students could portray their own family or the history of a family portrayed in children's literature.

▶ Draw upon stories such as *The Sky is Blue* by Charlotte Zolotow, *Hundred Penny Box* by Sharon E. Mathis, *Tell Me a Story* by Angela Johnson, and *They Were Good and Strong* by Robert Lawson to compare family life today with family life in the recent past.

▶ Compare the cultural similarities and differences in clothes, homes, food, communication, technology, cultural traditions, and other aspects of family life between families now and in the past. Possible sources might include information provided by family members, family photographs, artifacts, and books such as *The Keeping Quilt* by Patricia Polacco, *Thy Friend, Obadiah* by Burton Turkle, *From Me to You* by Paul Rogers, *The Patchwork Quilt* by Valerie Flournoy, and *The Old, Old Man and the Very Little Boy* by Kristine L. Franklin.

▶ Create charts, illustrations, Venn diagrams, or other graphic organizers to demonstrate similarities and differences between family life now and long ago.

▶ Draw upon literature such as *The House on Maple Street* by Bonnie Pryor or *Since 1920* by Alexandra Wallner to compare life in a home of the past with life in a community of the present. Create charts, illustrations, Venn diagrams, and other graphic organizers with examples of similarities and differences to demonstrate comparisons.

Grades 3-4

Examples of student achievement of Standard 1A include:

▶ Analyze daily life of a farm family from long ago in books such as *The Oxcart Man* by Donald Hall. Compare clothing, tools, and other aspects of life portrayed in the story with artifacts of that time (early 1800s) in a local museum; and role-play or create illustrations of various activities in the story such as going to market and selling produce.

▶ Through visits to "living history" sites such as the Strong Museum in Rochester, NY (a Victorian household), or Old Salem in North Carolina (colonial life), visits with senior citizens, interviews with reenactors, and records from local newspapers and historical societies, develop a mural, historical narrative, or dramatization of family life long ago.

▶ Examine a primary source such as a photograph or diary and formulate questions that they would like answered about family life in the past. Generate ideas about where to go to answer these questions.

*Girls reenacting a colonial pastime
in Williamsburg
Photograph courtesy of the
Colonial Williamsburg Foundation*

Students Should Be Able to:

1B Demonstrate understanding of the different ways people of diverse racial, religious, and ethnic groups, and of various national origins have transmitted their beliefs and values by:

K-4 Explaining the ways that families long ago expressed and transmitted their beliefs and values through oral traditions, literature, songs, art, religion, community celebrations, mementos, food, and language. [Obtain needed historical data]

3-4 Comparing the dreams and ideals that people from various groups have sought, some of the problems they encountered in realizing their dreams, and the sources of strength and determination that families drew upon and shared. [Compare and contrast]

Grades K-2

Examples of student achievement of Standard 1B include:

▶ Interview family members or older community members to discover and share stories, songs, and celebrations that are part of their family or cultural heritage.

▶ Draw upon stories such as *The Wooden Doll* by Susan Bonners, *Everybody Cooks Rice* by Norah Dooley, and *Corn Rows* by Camille Yarborough to compare ways in which people share family beliefs and values.

Grades 3-4

Examples of student achievement of Standard 1B include:

▶ Reenact, illustrate, or create stories describing ways various groups have transmitted beliefs and values through celebrations of national holidays, religious observances, and ethnic and national traditions (such as the Fourth of July, St. Patrick's Day, Christmas, Hanukkah, Yom Kippur, Kwanzaa, Chinese New Year, various Caribbean Independence Days, and Cinco de Mayo). Possible sources are: *An Early American Christmas* by Tomie DePaola, *Fiesta! Ethnic Traditional Holidays* by Jane Behrens, *One Little Goat: A Passover Song* edited by Marilyn Hirsh, *Pedro the Angel of Olvera Street* by Leo Politi, *Yussel's Prayer: A Yom Kippur Story* by Barbara Cohen, *Anni's India Diary* by Anni Axworthy, and *I Am a Musician* by Manju Aggarwal.

▶ Draw upon examples of visual arts and crafts in order to make generalizations about the values and beliefs of the people who made these things, now and long ago.

▶ Draw upon oral traditions, stories, and sacred literature of people from various groups in order to explain the beliefs transmitted through them. Possible sources are *Dancing Teepees: Poems of American Indian Youth* selected by Virginia Driving Haw Sneve, Bible stories, *Jataka* tales, *The People Could Fly* by Virginia Hamilton, and traditional literature from various countries. Whenever possible live performances and recordings should be presented to emphasize the oral tradition of these stories.

▶ Draw upon photographs of families long ago in various situations such as arriving in America and living together in a rural or urban setting in order to hypothesize how they maintained cultural beliefs: *What hopes and dreams did they have? What problems do you think they faced? What are some ways they might have used to keep strong in order to realize their dreams? What traditions did they bring from their cultural past?*

▶ Analyze the messages contained in poems, songs, short essays, and sayings that have been a source of inspiration and strength to people from various groups, e.g., Confucian sayings, hymns, Psalms and Proverbs from the Bible, poems like "Dreams" by Langston Hughes, W. E. B. Du Bois's *Advice to a Black School Girl*, and Ashley Bryan's *I'm Going to Sing*, a book of and about Negro spirituals.

Painting of the Sargent Family, 1800
Courtesy of the National Gallery of Art, Washington, D.C.

STANDARD 2

Students Should Understand: *The history of their own local community and how communities in North America varied long ago.*

Students Should Be Able to:

2A Demonstrate understanding of the history of their local community by:

`K-4` Creating a historical narrative about the history of their local community from data gathered from local residents, records found in early newspapers, historical documents and photographs, and artifacts and other data found in local museums and historical societies. [**Construct a historical narrative**]

`K-4` From resources that are available in the local community, recording changes that have occurred in goods and services over time. [**Establish temporal order**]

`K-4` Describing local community life long ago, including jobs, schooling, transportation, communication, religious observances, and recreation. [**Obtain needed historical data**]

`3-4` Interpreting population data from historical and current maps, charts, graphs, and census tables in order to make generalizations about the changing size and makeup of the local community. [**Interrogate the data**]

`K-4` Examining local architecture and landscape to compare changes in function and appearance over time. [**Draw upon visual data**]

`K-4` Identifying historical figures in the local community and explaining their contributions and significance. [**Assess the importance of the individual in history**]

`3-4` Identifying a problem in the community's past, analyzing the different perspectives of those involved, and evaluating choices people had and the solution they chose. [**Identify issues and problems in the past**]

Grades K-2

Examples of student achievement of Standard 2A include:

◆ Identify and compare changes in community life over time, such as those depicted in the books *The Little House* by Virginia Lee Burton, *The Changing City* and *The Changing Countryside* by Jorg Muller, *New Providence: A Changing Cityscape* by Renata von Tscharner, poems such as "Indian Children" in *Sung Under the Silver Umbrella* by Annette Wynne, or poster sets such as *Cityscapes* by Atheneum Press.

◆ Look at current photographs of the community to ask: *What things could have been here long ago? Why? What things look newer? Why?*

◆ Visit local museums, historic sites, and libraries as a family or classroom research project in order to create a booklet on "Life Long Ago."

◆ Read or view a history (book/movie) of the local community in order to group events into broad categories of historical time, such as "long, long ago," "yesterday," "today," and "tomorrow."

Grades 3-4

Examples of student achievement of Standard 2A include:

▶ Using primary sources found in local libraries and living history museums, create a time line of the history of the local community since its founding, including the people who came here, the changes they brought to the community, and significant events over time.

▶ From data obtained from early newspapers, catalogues, and narratives, chart differences between products and services now and long ago.

▶ Research a current issue in the community in which a historic site is threatened. Analyze the differing perspectives and develop a plan of action or proposal to resolve the issue. *What is the historical significance of the site?*

▶ Draw upon books such as *The Potato Man* by Megan McDonald and *In Coal Country* by Judith Hendershot, poems such as "The Village Blacksmith" by Longfellow, "I Hear America Singing" by Walt Whitman, "Honey I Love" and "The Children of Long Ago" by Eloise Greenfield, photographs and artifacts from local museums, newspapers, and historical societies to create a mural of images or 3-dimensional model representing the local community long ago.

▶ Explain changes in land use and economic activities in their local community since its founding. *How did changes in technology, for example, change the work people did in this community? What happened to their community when the railroad came through, when a new harbor or airport was built, a major highway bypassed the town, or a local resource was depleted?*

▶ Identify streets, buildings, and schools named after local citizens and research who they were and the role they played in the local community. Research other people who played an important role in the community in order to develop a historic argument in favor of naming a community site after them.

Blanche Lamont with students in her school, Hecla, Montana, 1893
Library of Congress

Students Should Be Able to:

2B   Demonstrate understanding of how communities in North America varied long ago by:

K-4 Comparing and contrasting the different ways in which early Hawaiian and Native American peoples such as the Iroquois, the Sioux, the Hopi, the Nez Perce, the Inuit, and the Cherokee adapted to their various environments and created their patterns of community life long ago. **[Compare and contrast differing sets of ideas]**

K-4 Drawing upon written and visual sources and describing the historical development and daily life of a colonial community such as Plymouth, Williamsburg, St. Augustine, San Antonio, and Post Vincennes, in order to create a historical narrative, mural, or dramatization of daily life in that place long ago. **[Construct a historical narrative]**

K-4 Describing the challenges and difficulties encountered by people in a pioneer farming community such as those found in the Old Northwest (e.g., Ohio), the prairies, the Southwest (e.g., Santa Fe), eastern Canada (e.g., Quebec), and the Far West (e.g., Salt Lake City). **[Read historical narratives imaginatively]**

3-4 Drawing upon maps and stories in order to identify geographical factors that led to the establishment and growth of communities such as mining towns (Sacramento) and trading settlements (New Orleans, Vincennes, and Astoria). **[Draw upon historical maps and read historical narratives imaginatively]**

3-4 Describing and comparing daily life in ethnically diverse urban communities long ago, such as a free African American community in Philadelphia, an Italian community in New York, or a Chinese community in San Francisco. **[Draw upon visual data and read historical narratives imaginatively]**

Grades K-2

Examples of student achievement of Standard 2B include:

▶ Draw upon stories that recount the myths, legends, and long-ago experiences of specific early Hawaiian or Native American peoples in order to draw pictures that illustrate the daily life and values of these cultures.

▶ Draw upon stories that describe life in a community of the past, such as *The Town That Moved* by Mary J. Fisand, *Sarah, Plain and Tall* by Patricia MacLachlan, and *Penny in the Road* by Katharine Wilson Precek, to create data retrieval charts, tables, or other graphic organizers.

Grades 3-4

Examples of student achievement of Standard 2B include:

▶ Pick topics of personal interest. Use maps, historical records, pictures, paintings (e.g., by Charles Russell, George Catlin) and student-generated questions to create a data retrieval chart comparing geographical features, economic activities, food, clothing, homes, crafts, and rituals of two or more Native American societies long ago.

▶ Draw upon stories such as *Williamsburg Household* by Joan Anderson in order to write a journal or diary entry depicting daily life in a colonial settlement, from the point of view of a child.

◗ Draw upon literature such as *Dakota Dugout* by Ann Turner, *Spanish Pioneers of the Southwest* by Joan Anderson, books by Laura Ingalls Wilder, tales of the frontier by Everett Dick, and photos in pictorial collections such as *Settlers in the American West* by Margaret Killingray and *The Black West* by William Loren Katz, in order to recount through stories, dramatizations, or paintings the hardships and difficulties encountered by people living in frontier communities.

◗ From information about a mining or trading community's relation to the geography of the area, create advertisements or handbills describing opportunities in the region and convincing people to come to the community for a particular purpose.

◗ Draw upon data in photographs of city life, fiction, and nonfiction, such as *Immigrant Kids* by Russell Freedman, and *Chinese Americans, Past and Present* by Don Wong and Irene Dea Collier, in order to write letters describing life in the community that a "city child" may have written to a relative in the country.

Children playing in front of an Italian market in Boston, ca. 1900
Library of Congress

TOPIC 2

The History of Students' Own State or Region

STANDARD 3

Students Should Understand: *The people, events, problems, and ideas that were significant in creating the history of their state.*

Students Should Be Able to:

3A Demonstrate understanding of the history of indigenous peoples who first lived in their state or region by:

K-4 Drawing upon data in paintings and artifacts to hypothesize about the culture of the early Hawaiians or Native Americans who are known to have lived in the state or region, e.g., the Anasazi of the Southwest, the Makah of the Northwest coast, the Eskimos/Inupiat of Alaska, the Creeks of the Southeast, the Mississippians (Cahokia), or the Mound Builders. [**Formulate historical questions**]

K-4 Drawing upon legends and myths of the Native Americans or Hawaiians who lived in students' state or region in order to describe personal accounts of their history. [**Read historical narratives imaginatively**]

3-4 Comparing and contrasting how Native American or Hawaiian life today differs from the life of these same groups over 100 years ago. [**Compare and contrast differing sets of ideas**]

Grades K-2

Examples of student achievement of Standard 3A include:

▶ Draw upon myths and legends such as *Arrow to the Sun* by Gerald McDermott, *How Man Slowed the Sun* by Suelyn Ching Tune, *Her Seven Brothers*, *Alaskan Igloo Tales* by Edward L. Keithahn, *Grandmother Stories: Indian Tales of the Northwest* by Nashone, *It Is Still That Way* by Bryd Baylor, and *How the Stars Fell into the Sky, A Navajo Legend* by Jerrie Oughton, in order to make a class picture of the origins and culture of the Native Americans or Hawaiians in the state.

▶ Examine artifacts found at museums, historical sites, or in pictures to generate questions and to hypothesize about early Hawaiian or Native American culture such as: *Who made this object? Why was it made? What could it have been used for? How was it made? What do the materials tell you about the environment?*

Grades 3-4

Examples of student achievement of Standard 3A include:

◗ Draw upon myths, legends, archaeological evidence, visits to historic sites, such as Angel Mounds State Historic Site (in southwestern Indiana), and pictures of artifacts to develop historical narratives about the origin and culture of the earliest inhabitants of the region or state.

◗ Draw upon books such as *Dogsong* by G. Paulson to compare the life and culture of Native Americans long ago and today.

Students Should Be Able to:

3B. **Demonstrate understanding of the history of the first European, African, and/or Asian-Pacific explorers and settlers who came to their state or region by:**

3-4 Gathering data in order to analyze geographic, economic, and religious reasons that brought the first explorers and settlers to the state or region. [**Obtain needed historical data**]

3-4 Reconstructing in time lines the order of early explorations and settlements including explorers, early settlements, and cities. [**Establish temporal order**]

K-4 Examining visual data in order to describe ways in which early settlers adapted to, utilized, and changed the environment. [**Draw upon visual data**]

3-4 Analyzing some of the interactions that occurred between the Native Americans or Hawaiians and the first European, African, and Asian-Pacific explorers and settlers in the students' state or region. [**Read historical narratives imaginatively**]

K-4 Using a variety of sources to construct a historical narrative about daily life in the early settlements of their state or region. [**Obtain needed historical data**]

Grades K-2

Examples of student achievement of Standard 3B include:

◗ Draw upon biographies of early explorers and books such as *Sarah Morton's Day* by Kate Waters, *Going West* by Jean Van Leuwen, and *On the Day Peter Stuyvesant Sailed into Town* by Arnold Lobel, in order to describe, either orally or visually, the life of early explorers and settlers.

◗ After visiting "living history" and other local museums, historic sites, and libraries, visually depict or develop a group story about daily life in early state history. (Encourage students to share information gained from family "field trips.")

Grades 3-4

Examples of student achievement of Standard 3B include:

◗ Make a picture map illustrating the people, places, and events of such early explorations of their state or region as those of Spanish explorers, French and English fur traders, Lewis and Clark, Marquette and Joliet, and James Beckwourth.

◗ Construct a historical map of the state or region locating early forts, missions, settlements, and cities.

▶ Draw upon data in historical maps, journals, and other available primary accounts and stories in order to describe why people came to their state or region long ago, and the effect the environment had on the location and establishment of early settlements (e.g., for fishing, hunting, farming, mining, trading, and milling).

▶ Draw upon stories such as *Aurora Means Dawn* by Scott Sanders, *The Courage of Sarah Noble* by Alice Dalgliesh, *Wagon Wheels* by Barbara Brenner; and primary source anecdotes such as, "There were so many trees in Ohio that a squirrel could hop from the Ohio River to Lake Erie without ever touching the ground" in order to write poems and diaries from the point of view of a child who first encounters a dense forest or expanse of prairie.

▶ Create a historical narrative, role play, dramatization, shoebox picture strip, or TV show depicting daily life in an early settlement from data available in source material such as *The Pilgrims of Plimoth* by Marcia Sewell, *The Jews of Amsterdam* and *The Early People of Florida* by Eva Deutsch Costabel, *Africa Remembered: Narratives by West Africans from the Era of the Slave Trade*, edited by Philip D. Curtin, *The Black Americans: A History in Their Own Words* by Milton Meltzer, *Diary of an Early American Boy, Noah Blake* by Eric Sloane, and *Readings in California History* by Ray and Gladys Gilmore.

▶ Draw upon stories and other sources that illustrate both exchange and conflict in order to analyze and reenact some of the early encounters between people of Native American, Hawaiian, European, Asian-Pacific, and African ancestry in their state or region. Sources depicting exchange include: *Squanto, Friend of the White Man* and *Pocahontas and the Strangers* by Clyde Bulla, *Conquista* by Scott O'Dell, and *Fur Trappers and Traders: The Indians, the Pilgrims, and the Beaver* by Beatrice Siegel. Sources depicting conflict include *Mary Jemison, Indian Captive* by Jeanne Le Mannier Gardner and biographies of the men and women who provided leadership during this period such as Black Hawk, Osceola, Tecumseh, Chief Joseph, Sitting Bull, Ninigret, Sacajawea, Mary Musgrove Bosomworth, Crazy Horse, Cochise, and Kamehameha. Poems by Stephen Vincent Benét in *Book of Americans* depict the reaction of Native Americans to the approach of the European ships.

Edward Hicks, Peaceable Kingdom
*Courtesy of the National Gallery
of Art, Washington, D.C.*

Students Should Be Able to:

3C Demonstrate understanding of the various other groups from regions throughout the world who came into the students' own state or region over the long-ago and recent past by:

`3-4` Developing a time line on their state or region and identifying the first inhabitants who lived there, each successive group of arrivals, and significant changes that developed over the history of their state or region. [**Establish temporal order**]

`K-4` Using a variety of visual data, fiction and nonfiction sources, and speakers to identify the groups that have come into the state or region and to generate ideas about why they came. [**Obtain needed historical data**]

`K-4` Examining photographs and pictures of people from the various racial and ethnic groups of varying socioeconomic status who lived in the state 100-200 years ago in order to hypothesize about their lives, feelings, plans, and dreams, and to compare ways in which their experiences were similar and different. [**Formulate historical questions**]

`3-4` Examining newspaper and magazine accounts and constructing interview questions for a written, telephone, or in-person interview with a recent immigrant in order to discover why they came, what their life was like, and to describe some of the experiences that they have had in adjusting to the state or region. [**Obtain needed historical data**]

`3-4` Draw upon census data and historical accounts in order to describe patterns and changes in population over a period of time in a particular city or town in the students' state or region. [**Draw upon needed historical data**]

`3-4` Describing the problems, including prejudice and intolerance, as well as the opportunities that various groups who have lived in their state or region have experienced in housing, the workplace, and the community. [**Evidence historical perspectives**]

`3-4` Drawing upon historical narratives to examine the sources of strength and determination, such as family, church, synagogue, community, or fraternal organizations that various groups drew upon in attempts to overcome problems during this period. [**Consider multiple perspectives**]

Grades K-2   **Examples of student achievement of Standard 3C include:**

▶ Draw upon stories about the experiences of immigrants in the recent past in order to retell the stories and discuss the good and bad experiences of the people who have moved into their state or region. Possible sources are *Angel Child, Dragon Child* by Michele Maria Surat, *The Land I Lost* by Hyunh Quang Nhoung, *Making a New Home in America* by Maxine Rosenberg, *How Many Days to America?* by Eve Bunting, *I Speak English for My Mom* by Muriel Stark, and *Grandfather's Journal* by Allen Say.

▶ Draw upon stories such as *The Drinking Gourd* by F.N. Monjo, *Next Spring an Oriole* by Gloria Whelan, *The Little Weaver of Thai-Yen Village* by Tran-Khanh-Tuyet, *Dancing with the Indians* by Angela Shelf Medearis, and *I Speak English For My Mom* by Muriel Stark in order to retell and analyze examples of people from different groups meeting, adjusting to, or helping one another. *What problems did they have? What did they do to overcome them? How would students suggest dealing with them and why?*

▶ Use newspaper accounts and literature to describe examples of how people from one cultural background have interacted with people from another. Possible fiction sources include *Halmoni and the Picnic* by Sook Nyul Choi, *I Hate English* by Ellen Levine, *I'm New Here* by Bud Howlett, and *The Day of the Rainbow* by Ruth Craft.

Grades 3-4

Examples of student achievement of Standard 3C include:

▶ Develop a time line of the history of their state or region, identify the original inhabitants living there, the times of arrival of those groups that came later, and the significant events and changes that developed in their state or region.

▶ Draw upon data provided by tables and graphs, fiction and nonfiction sources, and guest speakers in order to construct a graphic organizer comparing and contrasting the reasons various groups came to the state.

▶ Construct a mural or model of different types of settlements from various regions in the state including farm and sharecropping communities, small towns, and ethnic neighborhoods and centers of commerce and industry in which people lived and worked in big cities.

▶ Interpret photographs and historical narratives and stories that depict the obstacles encountered by various groups and their struggles to overcome them. Analyze a problem, considering the different perspectives of people involved, the options they had at the time for dealing with the problem, and the consequences of the decisions made. Possible sources include *Immigrant Kids* by Russell Freedman, *Strange New Feeling* by Julius Lester, *Immigrant Girl: Becky of Eldridge* by Brett Harvey, *Yonie Wondernose* by Marguerite De Angeli, *An Illustrated History of the Chinese in America* by Ruthanne L. McCunn, *The Black Americans: A History in Their Own Words* by Milton Meltzer, *Mexican in America* by Jane Pinchot, *Dimitry: A Young Soviet Immigrant* by Joanne E. Bermstoem, and *In the Year of the Boar* and *Jackie Robinson* by Bette Bao Lord.

▶ Use a world map to identify the national origins of the immigrants from various countries who have come to their state or region over the past 200 years. Color code movements by major periods of immigration in the history of their state or region.

▶ Draw upon personal interviews, oral histories, newspaper accounts, personal memoirs, census records, visual data, and other sources to create a talk show or newspaper describing the experiences of various recent immigrant groups in their state or region.

▶ Use census data for every 10 or 50 years (choose one fixed interval to view in succession) in order to graph patterns of migration to a particular city or town in the state.

Students Should Be Able to:

3D **Demonstrate understanding of the interactions among all these groups throughout the history of their state by:**

3-4 Listing in chronological order the major historical events that are part of the state's history. [**Establish temporal order**]

3-4 Analyzing the significance of major events in the state's history, their impact on people then and now, and their relationship to the history of the nation. [**Reconstruct the literal meaning of a passage**]

3-4 Reading historical narratives to describe how the territory or region attained its statehood. [**Reconstruct the literal meaning of a historical passage**]

3-4 Identifying historical problems or events in the state and analyzing the way they were solved and/or the ways that they continue to be addressed. [**Identify issues and problems in the past**]

3-4 Examining various written accounts in order to identify and describe regional or state examples of major historical events and developments that involved interaction among various groups (e.g., the Alamo, the Underground Railroad, the building of the Transcontinental Railroad, and the California Gold Rush. [**Consider multiple perspectives**]

3-4 Investigating the influence of geography on the history of the state or region and identifying issues and approaches to problems such as land use and environmental problems. [**Reconstruct the literal meaning of a historical passage**]

Grades K-2 | Examples of student achievement of Standard 3D include:

This Standard is probably not appropriate for young children.

Grades 3-4 | Examples of student achievement of Standard 3D include:

▶ Read historical narratives about important events or issues in the history of their state and analyze the context in which the event unfolded by answering questions such as: *What were the values or outlook of various people involved? What crisis or problems needed to be solved? What options did the people have? What were the motives, hopes, fears, strengths, and weaknesses of the people involved? What decisions were made in solving the problem? How would students recommend solving the problem, given the options available at that time? Why?*

▶ Create a pictorial time line depicting major historical events in the state's history, and add a parallel time line of related events occurring in the nation.

▶ Create a script, classroom newspaper, or historic debate to dramatize a significant event in the state's history.

▶ Draw upon fiction and nonfiction accounts dealing with major historical events and developments that involved different groups of people in the state or region (such as the Alamo, the Underground Railroad, the arrival of Christian missionaries in Hawaii and Junipero Serra in California, the California and Alaska Gold Rushes, post-Revolutionary War and post-Civil War migrations) in order to write a historical narrative recounting and explaining the interactions that occurred.

▶ Use a variety of sources to create a flow chart depicting a problem in the state's history, how it was solved, the people involved, and the results.

▶ Analyze some of the causes and effects (both positive and negative) of critical events or turning points in their state's history such as the closing of the missions in California, the "drying up" of silver mining in Colorado, the arrival of Lewis and Clark among the Mandan Indians, and the flood of European immigrants to New York around the turn of the century.

Students Should Be Able to:

3E **Demonstrate understanding of the ideas that were significant in the development of the state and that helped to forge its unique identity by:**

K-4 Drawing upon visual and other data to identify symbols, slogans, or mottoes, and researching why they represent the state. [**Draw upon visual data**]

3-4 Analyzing how the ideas of significant people affected the history of their state. [**Assess the importance of the individual in history**]

K-4 Researching in order to explain why important buildings, statues, monuments, and place names are associated with the state's history. [**Obtain needed historical data**]

3-4 Drawing upon a variety of sources to describe the unique historical conditions that influenced the formation of the state. [**Obtain needed historical data**]

Grades K-2

Examples of student achievement of Standard 3E include:

▶ Use pictures and other data to create a display of symbols, slogans, and mottoes, and label how they represent the state.

▶ Make a "big book" of buildings, statues, and monuments in the state's history.

Grades 3-4

Examples of student achievement of Standard 3E include:

▶ Examine a variety of sources that include biographies, reference material, primary source documents, and other nonfiction sources in order to write a speech about the ideas that played an important role in the history of the state.

▶ Research to discover the unique historical conditions that influenced the formation of the state, such as women's suffrage in Wyoming, the gold rush in California, and the Northwest Ordinance's influence on Wisconsin. Write a historical argument designed to convince the Congress of the United States to grant statehood to your area.

▶ Using a variety of resources, find examples of statues, monuments, important buildings, local schools, etc., named in honor of historical people. Explain why they were honored, and include the information in a student-made book about the state or region's history.

▶ Use a variety of resources to investigate the origin of the names of places, rivers, cities, and counties and explain the various cultural influences in a particular region.

Sketches from "Gleason's Pictorial" of a 19th-century California vaquero and a California miner
Library of Congress

T O P I C 3

The History of the United States: Democratic Principles and Values and the People from Many Cultures Who Contributed to Its Cultural, Economic, and Political Heritage

S T A N D A R D 4

Students Should Understand: *How democratic values came to be, and how they have been exemplified by people, events, and symbols.*

Students Should Be Able to:

4A Demonstrate understanding of how the United States government was formed and of the nation's basic democratic principles set forth in the Declaration of Independence and the Constitution by:

[K-4] Explaining that the U.S. government was formed by English colonists who fought for independence from England. [**Explain causes and consequences**]

[3-4] Identifying and explaining the basic principles that Americans set forth in the documents that declared the nation's independence from England (the Declaration of Independence) and that created the new nation's government (U.S. Constitution). [**Demonstrate and explain the influence of ideas**]

[K-4] Explaining the importance of the basic principles of American democracy that unify us as a nation: our individual rights to life, liberty, and the pursuit of happiness; responsibility for the common good; equality of opportunity and equal protection of the law; freedom of speech and religion; majority rule with protection for minority rights; and limitations on government, with power held by the people and delegated by them to their elected officials who are responsible to those who elected them to office. [Demonstrate and explain the influence of ideas]

[K-4] Analyzing how over the last 200 years indivudals and groups in American society have struggled to achieve the liberties and equality promised in the principles of American democracy. [**Analyze continuity and change**]

Grades K-2

Examples of student achievement of Standard 4A include:

▸ Draw upon stories and simple biographies of Revolutionary leaders such as George Washington, Thomas Jefferson, and Benjamin Franklin to explain their roles and importance in the Revolutionary War and the development of a new nation.

▸ Draw upon stories and simple biographies of Americans, ordinary and extraordinary, such as Rosa Parks, Martin Luther King Jr., Sojourner Truth, and César Chávez, who have worked to achieve equal rights and improve the lives of peoples of many groups.

Grades 3-4

Examples of student achievement of Standard 4A include:

▸ Draw upon such books as *Fourth of July Story* by Alice Dalgliesh and *Give Us Liberty: The Story of the Declaration of Independence* by Helen Peterson to explain the ideas in the Declaration of Independence.

▸ Draw upon biographies and stories of such leaders of the Revolutionary War as George Washington, Benjamin Franklin, and Thomas Jefferson to explain why Americans went to war to win independence from England.

▸ Analyze historical documents and stories of heroes during the Revolutionary War such as Nathan Hale and James Armistead who risked or gave their lives behind the British lines to obtain for George Washington urgently needed information of enemy troop strength and deployment.

▸ Develop a historical narrative, dramatization, or simulated interview with historic figures responsible for the Declaration of Independence and the U.S. Constitution and with leaders who have worked to guarantee these rights to all Americans in order to demonstrate the importance of the basic democratic principles set forth in these documents. *What are these principles and why have they been important to people, then and now? Why are they important in unifying a nation of people from many different national, religious, ethnic, racial, and cultural backgrounds? Why is it important that all people, whatever their backgrounds, share equally in the benefits of these basic democratic values?*

▸ Analyze a historical event or issue in their state or local community in which conflict arose over the equal rights of all citizens to the benefits guaranteed in the basic principles of American democracy: e.g., equal educational opportunity; nondiscriminatory housing; voting rights; access to public facilities; freedom of speech, the press, and religion; or equal justice under the law. *What right(s) were involved? How did the interests and beliefs of different persons involved in this issue differ? Was the conflict resolved fairly? Why or why not? What basic democratic values were preserved? abused? supported? How would you have recommended resolving the conflict and why?*

▸ Draw upon stories, biographies, and other sources to analyze how people have continued to struggle to bring to all groups in American society the liberties and equality promised in the basic principles of American democracy. *What was the importance of such leaders as Sojourner Truth, Harriett Tubman, Frederick Douglass, W. E. B. Du Bois, Booker T. Washington, Susan B. Anthony, Martin Luther King Jr., Rosa Parks, and César Chávez in this struggle?*

Students Should Be Able to:

4B Demonstrate understanding of ordinary people who have exemplified values and principles of American democracy by:

K-4 Identifying ordinary people who have believed in the fundamental democratic values such as justice, truth, equality, the rights of the individual, and responsibility for the common good, and explain their significance. [**Assess the importance of the individual in history**]

K-4 Analyzing in their historical context the accomplishments of ordinary people in the local community now and long ago who have done something beyond the ordinary that displays particular courage or a sense of responsibility in helping the common good. [**Assess the importance of the individual in history**]

Grades K-2

Examples of student achievement of Standard 4B include:

▶ Interview school personnel in order to identify the ways in which people, including other children, have helped the school in the past. Develop a solution for a current issue or problem in the school by applying such fundamental values as being fair, protecting individual rights, and being responsible for the common good.

▶ By visiting a police department, fire department, senior citizen home, or soup kitchen, or by inviting speakers in order to obtain data, describe and analyze how people have helped each other in the past in the community.

▶ Draw upon stories such as *Halmoni and the Picnic* by Sook Nyul Choi, interviews with family members, and members of local houses of worship and fraternal organizations to obtain data and report how people have helped newcomers get settled and learn the ways of our country.

Grades 3-4

Examples of student achievement of Standard 4B include:

▶ Draw upon fictionalized versions of real people in historical situations such as *Secret Soldier: The Story of Deborah Sampson* by Ann McGovern, *Susanna of the Alamo: A True Story* by John Jakes, and *Thunder at Gettysburg* by Patricia L. Gauch, in order to write a story about an ordinary person during a historical event. Other possible people to investigate might include: James Armistead, Sybil Ludington, Nathan Beman, Lydia Darragh, and Betty Zane.

▶ After reading about ordinary people in historic times, such as a Revolutionary War soldier, a suffragist, or a laborer in the early 1900s, write a diary entry from the point of view of that person explaining how he/she struggled for individual rights or for the common good. Possible sources might include books such as *Phoebe, the Spy* by Judith Berry Griffin, *Thee, Hannah* by Marguerite De Angeli, and *My Daddy Was a Soldier* by Deborah Kogan Ray.

▸ Use written material in local newspapers and newspaper archives, local libraries and historical societies, oral information obtained from members of the community, or trade books such as *A River Ran Wild* by Lynne Cherry, *Kate Shelly and the Midnight Express* by Margaret K. Wetterer, or *The Year of Fire* by Tedy Jam to create a display of "People who have helped make the community a better place to live." Possible areas to investigate are people who have worked to preserve the environment, to help the homeless, or to restore houses in low income areas.

▸ Analyze newspaper accounts of people in the recent past who have volunteered to help in unique situations, such as earthquakes, floods, and fires, and write journal entries from the perspective of those receiving the help.

Students Should Be Able to:

4C Demonstrate understanding of historic figures who have exemplified values and principles of American democracy by:

| K-4 | Identifying historical figures who believed in the fundamental democratic values such as justice, truth, equality, the rights of the individual, and responsibility for the common good, and explain their significance in their historical context and today. **[Assess the importance of the individual in history]**

| K-4 | Describing how historical figures in the United States and other parts of the world have advanced the rights of individuals and promoted the common good, and identifying character traits such as persistence, problem solving, moral responsibility, and respect for others that made them successful. **[Assess the importance of the individual in history]**

| 3-4 | Comparing historical biographies or fictionalized accounts of historical figures with primary documents in order to analyze inconsistencies and disagreements in these accounts, and assess their reliability. **[Compare competing historical narratives]**

Grades K-2

Examples of student achievement of Standard 4C include:

▸ Analyze stories and simple biographies of famous Americans, such as George Washington, Thomas Jefferson, Abraham Lincoln, Sojourner Truth, Susan B. Anthony, Mary McLeod Bethune, Eleanor Roosevelt, and Martin Luther King Jr., in order to explain how they reacted to their times and why they were significant in the history of our democracy. Possible sources might include: *A Picture Book of Martin Luther King, Jr.* by David A. Adler, *Mary McLeod Bethune: A Great Teacher* by Patricia and Fredrick McKissack, and *Benjamin Franklin* by Maggie Scarf.

▸ Explain the ways in which people in a variety of fields, such as Frederick Douglass, Clara Barton, Elizabeth Blackwell, Jackie Robinson, Rosa Parks, Jonas Salk, and César Chávez have advanced the cause of human rights, equality, and the common good.

▸ Place important figures that have been studied on a class time line, labeled with terms such as "long, long ago," "long ago," "yesterday," and "today."

Grades 3-4

Examples of student achievement of Standard 4C include:

- Draw upon such sources as historical literature, biographies, paintings, and photographs about a historical person and write a statement supported with anecdotes of the person's life to demonstrate why they think that person, in responding to issues or challenges of his or her time, exemplifies one or more democratic virtues, values, and characteristics.

- After reading a variety of biographies, explain why world figures such as Sun Yatsen, Mohandas Gandhi, Golda Meir, and Nelson Mandela exemplify democratic values such as equality and justice, and elaborate on what we can learn from them.

- Draw upon biographies and historical stories of such people as Richard Allen, Jane Addams, Dorothea Dix, John Muir, Susan LaFlesche, Mother Jones, Thurgood Marshall, and Roberto Clemente, who have fought for the rights of individuals, in order to identify the character traits that enabled them to overcome obstacles and fight successfully for the rights of others.

- Compare fictionalized stories such as *Mother, Aunt Susan, and Me* by William. J. Jacobs with historical photos and other primary sources on Susan B. Anthony and Elizabeth Cady Stanton and create a reenactment, news article, or story of their own concerning the struggle for women's suffrage.

- After reading from a variety of sources on one historical figure, analyze the similarities/differences in factual information, interpretation, or portrayal of character traits, author's style, validity of information, and sources used.

Students Should Be Able to:

4D Demonstrate understanding of events that celebrate and exemplify fundamental values and principles of American democracy by:

K-4 Describing the history of holidays, such as the birthday of Martin Luther King Jr., Presidents' Day, Memorial Day, the Fourth of July, Labor Day, Veterans' Day and Thanksgiving, that celebrate the core democratic values and principles of this nation. [Demonstrate and explain the influence of ideas]

3-4 Describing the history of events, such as the signing of the Mayflower Compact and the Declaration of Independence, and the writing of the Constitution, the Bill of Rights, and the Emancipation Proclamation. [Demonstrate and explain the influence of ideas and beliefs]

Grades K-2

Examples of student achievement of Standard 4D include:

- Draw upon sources such as *N.C. Wyeth's Pilgrims* by Robert San Souci, "The Emancipation Proclamation" from the Cornerstone of Freedom Series, *Fireworks, and Picnics and Flags: The Story of the Fourth of July Symbols* by James Cross Giblin in order to explain the reasons that America celebrates certain national holidays.

| Grades 3-4 | **Examples of student achievement of Standard 4D include:** |

◗ Develop a historical narrative, newspaper article, or other written account explaining the historical events and democratic values commemorated by major national holidays.

◗ Develop a historical narrative, dramatization, or simulated interview with historic figures responsible for such historical documents as the Mayflower Compact, the Declaration of Independence, the U.S. Constitution, the Bill of Rights, and the Emancipation Proclamation in order to demonstrate the significance of the document and its importance to people today.

Students Should Be Able to:

4E **Demonstrate understanding of national symbols through which American values and principles are expressed by:**

`K-4` Describing the history of American symbols such as the eagle, the Liberty Bell, George Washington as the "father of our country," and the national flag. [**Demonstrate and explain the influence of ideas**]

`K-4` Explaining why important buildings, statues, and monuments are associated with state and national history, such as the White House, Lincoln Memorial, Statue of Liberty, Ellis Island, Angel Island, Mt. Rushmore, and veterans memorials. [**Obtain needed historical data**]

`3-4` Analyzing the Pledge of Allegiance and patriotic songs, poems, and sayings that were written long ago to demonstrate understanding of their significance. [**Reconstruct the literal meaning of a historical passage**]

`3-4` Analyze songs, symbols, and slogans that demonstrate freedom of expression and the role of protest in a democracy. [**Consider multiple perspectives**]

| Grades K-2 | **Examples of student achievement of Standard 4E include:** |

◗ Draw upon sources such as coins, photographs of the Great Seal with the American Eagle, the Liberty Bell, the national flag, paintings by Charles Wilson Peale, and poetry and stamped images of George Washington that portray him as "father of our country" in order to develop a class "big book" of American symbols reinforcing the idea of one nation.

◗ Draw upon stories such as *The Story of the Statue of Liberty* by Betty Maestro and *Miss Liberty: First Lady of the World* by June Behrens in order to explain the idea that the statue represents.

◗ Draw upon stories such as *I Pledge Allegiance* by Juen Swanson, *Did You Carry the Flag Today, Charlie?* by Rebecca Caudill, and *The Story of the Star Spangled Banner* (Cornerstones of Freedom series), as well as photographs of historic occasions where the flag was raised, such as Iwo Jima and the moon landing, in order to analyze the importance and inspiration that the flag has been to people in the past.

▶ Draw upon books such as *How They Built the Statue of Liberty* by Mary J. Shapiro and *The Inside Outside Book of Washington, D.C.* by Roxie Munro in order to explain the historic importance of particular buildings, statues, and monuments in our country.

Grades 3-4

Examples of student achievement of Standard 4E include:

▶ Draw upon the plans and surveys for Washington, D.C. by Benjamin Banneker and Pierre L'Enfant and historical anecdotes about the White House such as Dolly Madison's saving of George Washington's portrait during the British burning of Washington in order to produce a documentary or "talk show" set in the past and analyze such questions as: *Why did we decide to have a new city for our government? Why is it important to have a White House?* Helpful sources may be *The White House* by Leonard Edward Fisher or *The Story of the White House* by Kate Waters.

▶ Explain how ordinary people have worked to contribute money and ideas to create or enhance our national symbols. Possible topics to investigate might include how French school children raised money for the Statue of Liberty and how Lee Iaccoca worked to restore Ellis Island.

▶ Analyze the words and explain the meaning of such songs as "America the Beautiful," "The Star Spangled Banner," and "My Country 'Tis of Thee."

▶ Examine pictures and videos, conduct interviews, and utilize other sources to create a "museum display" that includes songs, buttons, slogans, political cartoons, news accounts, photos, and other displays depicting the importance of freedom of speech and the role of protest in America. *How have these rights to free speech and protest been used to further such values as individual liberties, civil rights, equality, and economic opportunity?* Possible topics to investigate might include the Boston Tea Party, the abolition of slavery, women's suffrage, labor movements, and the civil rights movement.

*Children display a quilt they made commemorating American Women of Achievement
Photograph by Lee Simmons, 75th Street Elementary School, Los Angeles, CA*

STANDARD 5

Students Should Understand: *The causes and nature of various movements of large groups of people into and within the U.S., now and long ago.*

Students Should Be Able to:

5A Demonstrate understanding of the movements of large groups of people into their own and other states in the U.S. now and long ago by:

[3-4] Drawing upon data in historical maps, historical narratives, diaries, and other fiction or nonfiction accounts in order to chart various movements (westward, northward, and eastward) in the United States. [**Obtain needed historical data**]

[K-4] Gathering data in order to describe the forced relocation of Native Americans and how their lives, rights, and territories were affected by European colonization and the expansion of the United States, including examples such as Spanish colonization in the Southwest, Tecumseh's resistance to Indian removal, Cherokee Trail of Tears, Black Hawk's War, and the movement of the Nez Perce. [**Obtain needed historical data**]

[K-4] Drawing upon data from charts, historical maps, nonfiction and fiction accounts, and interviews in order to describe "through their eyes" the experience of immigrant groups. Include information such as where they came from and why they left, travel experiences, ports of entry and immigration screening, and the opportunities and obstacles they encountered when they arrived in America. [**Evidence historical perspectives**]

[3-4] Identifying reasons why groups such as freed African Americans, Mexican and Puerto Rican migrant workers, and Dust Bowl farm families migrated to various parts of the country. [**Consider multiple perspectives**]

[3-4] Analyzing the experiences of those who moved from farm to city during the periods when cities grew rapidly in the United States. [**Read historical narratives imaginatively**]

Grades K-2

Examples of student achievement of Standard 5A include:

▶ Draw upon stories of people who moved from faraway places to the U.S., in order to identify and describe the changes that occur in people's lives when they move, now and long ago. Possible sources are *The Remembering Box* by Eth Clifford, *How Far Felipe?* by Genevieve Gray, *Molly's Pilgrim* by Barbara Cohen, *The King of Prussia and the Peanut Butter Sandwich* by Alice Fleming, *Tales From a Gold Mountain* by Paul Yee, and *Addie Across the Prairie* by Laurie Lawson.

▶ Analyze what life was like for children and families "on the trail" by listening to stories such as *The White Stallion* by Elizabeth Shub, role-play episodes of life in the wagon train, illustrate episodes from the story, and locate the trail on a map of Texas from the 1840s.

Grades 3-4

Examples of student achievement of Standard 5A include:

▶ Draw upon data in maps and historical accounts in order to chart the major movements of peoples in the 19th-century expansion of the U.S.

▶ Select and use appropriate reference material and stories and computer software to hypothesize about the dreams, hopes, and reasons that people moved, and to answer such research questions as *"Why did people move to the West long ago in America?"* (Consider movements northward from Mexico and eastward from Asia as well as westward from eastern states in the movement of people into the present-day western U.S.) Possible sources are *The Pioneers Go West* by George Stewart; *Grasshopper Summer* by Ann Turner; and the photo collection, *The Black West*, by William Lorent Katz.

▶ Develop a packing list for a move from east to west, from south to north, or from farms to the city. Write a diary account of the journey that includes a map. Possible sources are *Overland to California in 1859: A Guide for Wagon Train Travellers* by Louis Block, and *If You Travelled West in a Covered Wagon* by Ellen Levine.

▶ Interpret paintings of buffalo herds and hunts by William Jacob Hays and Charles Russell (Cobblestone, 1990) and read sources that depict Indian removal such as *Only the Tears Remain*; *The Cherokees and the Trail of Tears*; *Native American Testimony: An Anthology of Indian and White Relations*; and *Indian Oratory: Famous Speeches by Noted Indian Chieftains* in order to create a diary or give a speech from a Native American's point of view of the coming of the new settlers.

▶ Draw upon appropriate references and stories such as *Chang's Paper Pony* by Eleanor Coerr, *Watch the Stars Come Out* by Riki Levinson, *Call Me Ruth* by Marilyn Sachs, and *Samurai of Gold Hill* by Toshiko Uchida in order to answer research questions such as: *What were some big changes experienced by immigrants who came to America long ago?*

▶ Draw upon data from pictures of sharecropping families and farms, and stories such as *Strange New Feeling* by Julius Lester, *The Gold Cadillac* by Mildred Taylor, *Nettie's Trip South* by Ann Turner, and *The Great Migration: An American Story* by Jacob Lawrence in order to hypothesize about the reasons why people would want to move in search of a better life, and compare this to experiences in students' own lives.

▶ Compare maps that show the number of big cities in 1850 and 1900 in the U.S., and hypothesize why people moved to these cities.

A nester family, Three Rock Ranch near Richardson, New Mexico
Library of Congress

STANDARD 6

Students Should Understand: *Folklore and other cultural contributions from various regions of the U.S. and how they help to form a national heritage.*

Students Should Be Able to:

6A Demonstrate understanding of folklore and other cultural contributions from various regions of the U.S. and how they help to form a national heritage by:

K–4 Describing regional folk heroes, stories, or songs that have contributed to the development of the cultural history of the U.S. [**Read historical narratives imaginatively**]

K–4 Drawing upon a variety of stories, legends, songs, ballads, games, and tall tales in order to describe the environment, lifestyles, beliefs, and struggles of people in various regions of the country. [**Read historical narratives imaginatively**]

3–4 Examining art, crafts, music, and language of people from a variety of regions long ago and describing their influence on the nation. [**Draw upon visual and other needed historical data**]

Grades K-2

Examples of student achievement of Standard 6A include:

▶ After listening to or reading stories of tricksters and tall tale heroes, such as Pecos Bill, Brer Rabbit, Paul Bunyan, Davey Crockett, John Henry, and Joe Magarac make a fact/fiction picture book.

▶ React to stories, storytellers, dances and music by participating in singing and dancing to various folksongs and dances. Possible sources are *Mirandy and Brother Wind* by P. McKissak and *The Diane Goode Book of American Folk Tales and Songs* by Anne Dorell.

▶ Compare the toys and games that children played long ago with the toys and games of today.

Grades 3-4

Examples of student achievement of Standard 6A include:

▶ After reading stories of tall tale heroes from various regions, chart them according to hero, setting, things he or she did, and exaggerations. Formulate generalizations from the chart based on questions such as: *Are the deeds any different from what ordinary people tried to do in their everyday lives? Why were many deeds associated with taming weather, wilderness, animals, rivers, and even slave masters? What do we know about people from their stories and heroes? Why do you think they told and retold such stories?*

◗ Reenact the stories of real people who became legends in their state, using regional dialects, sayings, colloquialisms, props, and costumes. Examples might include such people as frontiersmen (Daniel Boone, Simon Kenton), cowboys (Nat Love), mountain men (Jim Beckwourth, Jedediah Smith), American Indian chiefs (Geronimo), outlaws (Billy the Kid and Tiburcio Vásquez), and other popular figures (Annie Oakley, Johnny Appleseed, and Harriet Tubman).

◗ Analyze how poems and songs that were written long ago reflect the history of various regions and have contributed to our cultural heritage. Examples of songs include: "On Top of Old Smokey," "Home on the Range," "I've Been Working on the Railroad," "Old Chisholm Trail," "Erie Canal," and "Clementine." Examples of poetry include: "Hiawatha" (Longfellow), "When the Frost is on the Punkin" (James Whitcomb Riley), "Candle-Lightin' Time" (Paul Lawrence Dunbar), and "Brother Eagle, Sister Sky" (Chief Seattle).

◗ Draw upon various sources of folklore that can be gained from local archives, museums, fraternal organizations, churches, and local societies that reflect various ethnic, cultural, and religious backgrounds in order to produce a class culture festival. Possible book sources include: *Dr. Coyote: A Native American Aesop's Fables* by John Bierhorst, *The Jack Tales* by Richard Chase, *The Pennsylvania Dutch: Craftsmen and Farmers* by Eva Deutsch Costabel, *The Tales of Uncle Remus: The Adventures of Brer Rabbit* by Julius Lester, *Where Indians Live: American Indian Houses* by Nashone, *American Tall Tales* by Mary Pope Osborne, *You and Me and the Heritage Tree: Children's Crafts From 21 American Traditions* by Phyllis Fecrotte, *I'm Going to Sing: Black America — Spirituals*, Volume II by Ashley Bryan; and *From Sea to Shining Sea: A Treasury of American Folklore and Folk Songs* compiled by Amy L. Cohn.

Teachers at the Baltimore Great Blacks in Wax Museum Photograph courtesy of Dr. Samuel Banks Baltimore City Schools

Photograph by Leslie Slavin
Courtesy of the American Association
of School Librarians/ALA

Photograph by Bert Seal
San Diego County Office of Education

T O P I C 4

The History of Peoples of Many Cultures Around the World

S T A N D A R D   7

Students Should Understand: *Selected attributes and historical developments of societies in such places as Africa, the Americas, Asia, and Europe.*

Students Should Be Able to:

7A **Demonstrate understanding of the cultures and historical developments of selected societies in such places as Africa, the Americas, Asia, and Europe by:**

`3-4` Investigating the ways historians learn about the past if there are no written records. **[Compare records from the past]**

`3-4` Describing the effects geography has had on societies, including their development of urban centers, food, clothing, industry, agriculture, shelter, trade, and other aspects of culture. **[Draw upon historical maps]**

`K-4` Comparing and contrasting various aspects of family life, structures, and roles in different cultures and in many eras with students' own family lives. **[Compare and contrast]**

`K-4` Illustrating or retelling the main ideas in folktales, legends, myths, and stories of heroism that disclose the history and traditions of various cultures around the world. **[Reconstruct the literal meaning]**

`3-4` Describing life in urban areas and communities of various cultures of the world at various times in their history. **[Obtain needed historical data]**

`3-4` Describing significant historical achievements of various cultures of the world. **[Obtain needed historical data]**

`K-4` Analyzing the dance, music, and the arts of various cultures around the world to draw conclusions about the history, daily life, and beliefs of the people in history. **[Draw upon visual data]**

`K-4` Explaining the customs related to important holidays and ceremonies in various countries in the past. **[Assess the importance of ideas and beliefs in history]**

| Grades K-2 | **Examples of Student Achievement of Standard 7A include:** |

▶ Retell (using a beginning, middle, and end) and illustrate folktales, stories of great heroism, fables, legends, and myths that disclose beliefs and ways of living of various cultures in times past. Possible sources include *Belling the Cat and Other Aesop's Fables* retold by Tom Paxton, Bible stories such as David and Goliath, *Song of the Chirimia: A Guatemalan Folktale* retold by Jane Ann Volkman, *The Seven Chinese Brothers* by Margaret Maby, *Cyclops* by Leonard Everett Fisher, *Tower to Heaven* retold by Ruby Dee, and other stories from around the world.

▶ Analyze the visual images of people, places, and landmarks from long ago in books such as *Anno's Britain* and *Anno's Italy* by Mitsumasa Anno.

▶ After reading various stories and books about holidays and ceremonies, such as a 19th-century Christmas celebration in Scandinavia, Germany, or England; Cinco de Mayo; the Chinese New Year; the Japanese tea ceremony; and harvest and spring festivals, draw pictures, create relevant objects, or dramatize aspects of the celebration.

▶ Draw upon paintings, sculptures, masks, and other art forms to hypothesize and formulate questions about daily life and beliefs in various historical societies.

| Grades 3-4 | **Examples of student achievement of Standard 7A include:** |

▶ Draw upon data to analyze the effects of the geographic environment on the location, development, and activities of early societies, such as how rivers affected farming in China and Egypt, how the mountains affected farming in Peru, how the location of natural resources affected trade in Africa, and how the Mediterranean Sea enabled trading in Greece and neighboring regions. Possible sources might include *On the Banks of the Pharaoh's Nile* by Corinne Courtalon, *Llama and the Great Flood: A Folktale of Peru* by Ellen Alexander, and computer and CD-ROM software.

▶ Draw upon legends, myths, and hero tales from ancient and medieval times to analyze the heroism, courage, and loyalty expressed in such legends as: *The Minotaur* and *Ulysses and the Cyclops* retold by Andrew Lang; and hero tales retold by James Baldwin such as *The Brave Three Hundred,* the story of Sparta's stand at Thermopylae against the Persians; *Horatio at the Bridge; Crossing the Rubicon,* a story of Julius Caesar; *The Story of Regulus,* a legend from the Punic Wars; *The Story of Cincinnatus,* a legend of loyalty from ancient Rome; and *William Tell,* a legend of the 14th-century Swiss struggle for independence.

▶ Draw upon books and stories such as *A Medieval Feast* by Aliki, *The Village of Round and Square Houses* by Ann Grifalconi and *Inside a Roman Town* by Jonathan Rutland, in order to create a historical narrative or role-play a day in the life of a family in different eras of history.

▶ Compare and contrast various family structures, such as matrilineal families in some African societies and the extended families in China.

▶ Dramatize or retell literary selections that describe the historical memories, traditions and beliefs of various ancient societies such as Greek, Mayan, Norse and Arabic myths; stories from the Hebrew Bible such as "The Long, Hard Way Through the Wilderness," the story of the Hebrews' exodus from Egypt, retold by Walter Russell Bowie; and "How Queen Esther Saved Her People," retold by Walter Russell Bowie; a children's version of such classics as Virgil's *Aeneid,* Homer's *Odyssey,* or Sophocles' *Antigone;* and *Jataka* tales from India.

▶ Make a visual or model to compare life in a historic urban center, such as ancient Rome, Tenochtitlán, Timbuktu, or a medieval city, with the student's own community.

▶ Create models, diagrams, or pictures depicting significant architectural achievements in various historical societies such as the Hanging Gardens in Babylon, the Taj Mahal in India, pyramids in Egypt, temples in ancient Greece, and bridges and aqueducts in ancient Rome.

Students Should Be Able to:

7B Demonstrate understanding of great world movements of people now and long ago by:

3-4 Tracing on maps and explaining the migrations of large groups, such as the movement of Native American ancestors across the Bering Strait land bridge, the Bantu migrations in Africa, the movement of Europeans and Africans to the Western Hemisphere, and the exodus of Vietnamese boat people, Haitians, and Cubans in recent decades. **[Obtain needed historical data]**

K-4 Drawing upon historical narratives to identify early explorers and world travelers, such as Marco Polo, Zheng He, Eric the Red, and Christopher Columbus, and to describe the knowledge gained from their journeys. **[Read historical narratives imaginatively]**

K-4 Drawing upon historical narratives in order to identify European explorers of the 15th and 16th centuries, and explaining their reasons for exploring, the information gained from their journeys, and what happened as a result of their travels. **[Obtain needed historical data and read historical narratives imaginatively]**

3-4 Gathering data in order to explain the effects of the diffusion of food crops and animals between the Western and Eastern hemispheres after the voyages of Columbus. **[Obtain historical data]**

Grades K-2

Examples of student achievement of Standard 7B include:

▶ Draw upon historical narratives of the journeys of Marco Polo and Christopher Columbus, such as *The Journal of Marco Polo*, in order to create "Big Books" of images and maps showing the routes these travelers took and their descriptions of sites and events.

Grades 3-4

Examples of student achievement of Standard 7B include:

▶ Draw upon stories to create a world map locating great migrations of people in the past, such as the movement of Native Americans southward and eastward across the Americas following their early arrival via the Bering Strait land bridge and the great Bantu migrations in Africa.

▶ Draw upon appropriate sources in order to answer historical questions about great population movements in history, such as: *What reasons have caused large groups of people to move? What forms of transportation have been used to move long distances at various times in history? How did life change for these people as they moved to new environments?*

◗ Draw upon paintings, drawings, and models of early sailing ships and navigational instruments, maps, and charts to tell the story of the voyages of exploration that carried Europeans to Africa, Asia, and the Americas, and launched one of the great population movements in history. A possible source is *How We Learned the Earth is Round* by Patricia Lauber.

◗ From data they have researched concerning major explorers, such as Marco Polo, Christopher Columbus, Henry Hudson, Ferdinand Magellan, Vasco da Gama, and Jacques Cartier, write biographies including answers to historical questions such as: *What were they looking for? What did they use as transportation? What events occurred during the voyages? What did the people in these regions think about the explorers, how did they react to them, and what were the consequences (for both)?*

◗ Draw upon books such as *The Great Atlas of Discovery* by Neil Grant and other visual data on expeditions in order to create maps or map overlays of routes and destinations of early explorers.

◗ Chart with images and information the various crops, foods, and animals that moved from the Western Hemisphere (such as the tomato, corn, cassava, and potato) and from the Eastern Hemisphere (such as the horse, cattle, and sugarcane) as a result of the "Columbian Exchange."

◗ Read from a variety of sources such as *Encounter* by Jane Yolen to determine the different perspectives surrounding the Columbian encounter and stage a debate raising some of the major arguments.

Shipboard life
Illustrated by Sharon Rudahl

STANDARD 8

Students Should Understand: *Major discoveries in science and technology, some of their social and economic effects, and the major scientists and inventors responsible for them.*

Students Should Be Able to:

8A Demonstrate understanding of the development of technological innovations, the major scientists and inventors associated with them and their social and economic effects by:

K-4 Comparing and contrasting the behaviors of hunters and gatherers with those of people who cultivated plants and raised domesticated animals for food. [**Compare and contrast differing sets of ideas**]

K-4 Drawing upon visual data to illustrate development of the wheel and its early uses in ancient societies. [**Demonstrate and explain the influence of ideas**]

3-4 Describing the development and the influence of basic tools on work and behavior. [**Demonstrate and explain the influence of ideas**]

3-4 Identifying and describing various technological developments to control fire, water, wind, and soil, and to utilize natural resources such as trees, coal, oil, and gas in order to satisfy the basic human needs for food, water, clothing, and shelter. [**Obtain needed historical data**]

3-4 Identifying and describing technological inventions and developments that evolved during the 19th century and the influence of these changes on the lives of workers. [**Demonstrate and explain the influence of ideas**]

K-4 Identifying and describing the significant achievements of important scientists and inventors. [**Assess the importance of the individual in history**]

Grades K-2

Examples of student achievement of Standard 8A include:

▶ Draw upon visual data and field trips to local museums in order to write a story or draw a picture that explains the changes in family life that occurred when the family no longer had to hunt for food, could be supported on smaller amounts of land, and could acquire surplus food for storage and trading.

▶ After reading simple biographies, create a portrait of a famous person with props that represent the important accomplishments of that person, such as George Washington Carver with a peanut, Galileo with a telescope, Marie Curie with a test tube, Louis Pasteur with a glass of milk, and Alexander Graham Bell with a telephone.

Grades 3-4

Examples of student achievement of Standard 8A include:

▶ Create a picture time line tracing the development of the wheel and simple tools in the ancient world, and subsequent developments in technological inventions, control of the elements, and work.

▶ Make an annotated picture book or scrapbook that describes significant scientific and technological achievements in various historical societies, such as the invention of paper in China, Mayan calendars, mummification in Egypt, astronomical discoveries in the Moslem world, and the invention of the steam engine in England.

▶ Examine appropriate reference and fiction and nonfiction resources, such as *How Things Work* by David Macaulay and *The Great Wall of China* by Leonard Everett Fisher in order to develop a list or make replicas of basic tools and simple machines, and answer such research questions as: *What are some tools and devices that have been invented to make life easier?* or *How did the earliest developments in tools and machines influence social and economic life?*

▶ Select and use appropriate reference materials, such as the February 1992 issue of *Cobblestone* magazine, the book *Black Inventors and Their Inventions* by Jim Haskins, historical narratives, a variety of biographies on inventors, and computer and CD-ROM software in order to answer the research questions: *In what ways did the Industrial Revolution affect the lives of crafts people in the 19th century? What are the individual character traits that were necessary to bring about the explosion of inventions that occurred during the industrial revolution?* (Another possible source is *Created Equal, The Lives and Ideas of Black American Innovators* by James Michael Brodie.)

Chinese officials in a carriage
Illustrated by Carole Collier Frick

Students Should Be Able to:

8B Demonstrate understanding of changes in transportation and their effects by:

3-4 Creating a time line showing the varieties in forms of transportation and their developments over time. [**Create time lines**]

K-4 Drawing upon photographs, illustrations, models, and nonfictional resource materials to demonstrate the developments in marine vessels constructed by people from ancient times until today. [**Reconstruct patterns of historical succession and duration**]

3-4 Investigating the development of extensive road systems, such as the Roman roads of the early Roman Empire; the trade routes by camel caravan linking East Asia, Southwest Asia, and Africa during the ancient and early Middle Ages; the network of roads and highways of the Incas in Peru; the National Road in the U.S.; and the interstate highway system in order to explain the travel and communication difficulties encountered by people over vast expanses of territory, and the social and economic effects of these developments. [**Obtain needed historical data**]

3-4 Tracing the developments in rail transportation beginning in the 19th century and the effects of national systems of railroad transport on the lives of people. [**Reconstruct patterns of historical succession and duration.**]

3-4 Investigating the design and development of aircraft and rocketry and the people involved. [**Reconstruct patterns of historical succession and duration**]

3-4 Identifying and describing the people who have made significant contributions in the field of transportation. [**Assess the importance of the individual in history**]

Grades K-2

Examples of student achievement of Standard 8B include:

▶ Compare and contrast differences in the methods of travel from various times in human history and the comparative advantages and disadvantages of each, including, for example, the use of animals such as horses, llamas, camels, and elephants; nonmotorized vehicles such as chariots, travoises, bicycles, blimps, hot air balloons, and gliders; motorized transport such as railroads, motorcycles, automobiles, electric rail systems, and airplanes; and modern space advances.

▶ Analyze the illustrations in books such as *Erie Canal* by Peter Spier and describe the technology and activities of people along the canal.

▶ Use an artifact such as a horseshoe to generate thinking and answer questions such as: *What is this? Was it ever used around our school? What does it have to do with transportation?*

Grades 3-4

Examples of student achievement of Standard 8B include:

▶ Create from data concerning the development of marine vessels throughout history a time line or pictorial map of the world depicting the variety of ships used, the name of the place or individuals associated with them, the date when their use was first recorded, and any special features or uses of the ships. Examples might include such ships as the early dugout Phoenician ships, Native America canoes, the Portuguese caravel, the Chinese vessels used by Zheng He, the Arab dhow, the

Norse long ships, currachs used in the British Isles, square-riggers, aircraft carriers, submarines, and bathyscaphs.

▸ Gather data from charts, historical maps, and nonfiction resources in order to answer research questions, such as: *How did highway and road systems develop in earlier societies? How did complex highway and road systems facilitate movement and communication between distant locations? How did the building of national systems of railroads change the lives and work of people in Europe, Africa, Asia, and the Americas in the 19th century? How has the decline of the passenger rail system changed cities and towns in America?*

▸ Research famous "trailblazers" such as Henry Ford, Amelia Earhart, John Glenn, and Sally Ride in order to dramatize a mock interview with one of these people that discloses their achievements and assesses the importance of their work for people then and now.

Students Should Be Able to:

8C Demonstrate understanding of changes in communication and their effects by:

[K-4] Comparing and contrasting ways people communicate with each other now and long ago, and listing in chronological order technological developments that facilitated communication. [**Establish temporal order**]

[3-4] Illustrating the origins and changes in methods of writing over time and describing how the changes made communication between people more effective. [**Obtain needed historical data**]

[3-4] Explaining the significance of the printing press, the computer, and electronic developments in communication, and describing their impact on the spread of ideas. [**Obtain needed historical data**]

[K-4] Comparing and contrasting various systems of long-distance communication, including runners, the "talking drums" of Africa, smoke signals of Native Americans, the pony express, the telegraph, telephones, and satellite systems of worldwide communication today, and analyzing their effects. [**Compare and contrast**]

[3-4] Identifying and describing the people who have made significant contributions in the field of communication. [**Assess the importance of the individual**]

Grades K-2 — Examples of student achievement of Standard 8C include:

▸ Draw upon a variety of sources, such as *How Things Work* by David Macaulay, in order to create a picture time line of "How Communication Has Improved Over Time," including such methods as speaking by gestures, transmitting stories orally, pictographs, hieroglyphics, different alphabets, writing by hand, printing techniques, the invention of the telegraph and telephone, and satellite transmission of messages.

▸ Compare various ways people communicated over long distances before the invention of the telephone and telegraph, including runners, the "talking drums" of Africans, smoke signals of some Native Americans, and the pony express.

Grades 3-4

Examples of student achievement of Standard 8C include:

▸ Make a chart showing the origin of writing, including pictographs, cuneiform in which symbols were simplified, hieroglyphics, and alphabets in which each symbol stood for a sound; and describe the effects of the changes on early societies.

▸ Analyze the invention of the printing press with movable type in its effects on the spread of ideas, and answer the question: *Why is Gutenberg sometimes called the inventor who changed the world?*

▸ Read biographies of inventors and other nonfiction sources to analyze the significance of such inventions as the Braille alphabet, the telephone, the telegraph, radio, television, the computer, and satellite communication. *How have they changed the world? Are people better off or not as a consequence of these developments?*

Photograph by Bert Seal
San Diego County Office of Education

Contributors and Participating Organizations

Participating Organizations

American Association of School Librarians

American Association for State and Local History

American Federation of Teachers

American Historical Association

Association for the Study of Afro-American Life and History

Association for Supervision and Curriculum Development

The Atlantic Council of the United States

Center for Civic Education

Council for American Private Education

Council for Basic Education

Council of Chief State School Officers

Council of the Great City Schools

Council of State Social Studies Specialists

Educational Excellence Network

League of United Latin American Citizens

Lutheran Schools, The Lutheran Church-Missouri Synod

National Alliance of Black School Educators

National Association for Asian and Pacific American Education

National Association of Elementary School Principals

National Association of Secondary School Principals

National Association of State Boards of Education

National Catholic Educational Association

National Congress of Parents and Teachers

National Council for Geographic Education

National Council for History Education

The National Council for the Social Studies

National Council on Economic Education

National Education Association

Native American Heritage Commission

Organization of American Historians

Organization of History Teachers

Quality Education for Minorities Network

Social Science Education Consortium

Organizational Structure of the National History Standards Project

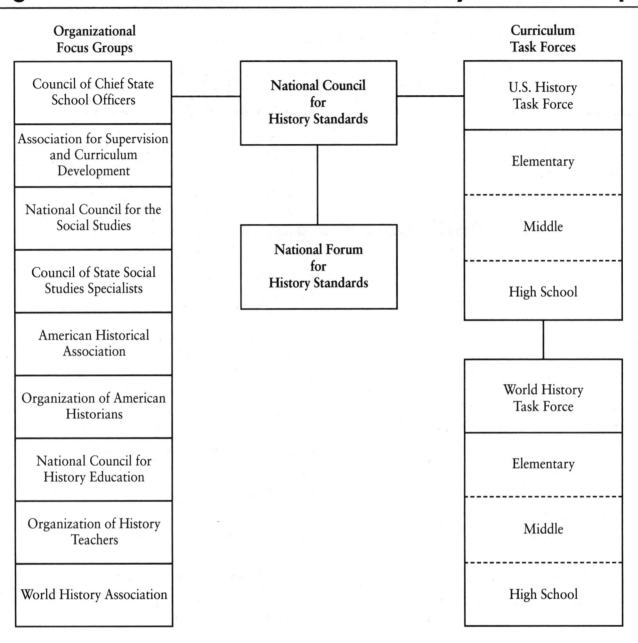

Organizational
Focus Groups

Council of Chief State
School Officers

Association for Supervision
and Curriculum
Development

National Council for the
Social Studies

Council of State Social
Studies Specialists

American Historical
Association

Organization of American
Historians

National Council for
History Education

Organization of History
Teachers

World History Association

National Council
for
History Standards

National Forum
for
History Standards

Curriculum
Task Forces

U.S. History
Task Force

Elementary

Middle

High School

World History
Task Force

Elementary

Middle

High School

Organizational Rosters

National Council for History Standards

Officers

Charlotte Crabtree, Co-Chair
Professor of Education Emeritus
University of California, Los Angeles

Gary B. Nash, Co-Chair
Professor of History
University of California, Los Angeles

Linda Symcox, Coordinator
Associate Director, National Center for History in the Schools
University of California, Los Angeles

Members

Charlotte Anderson, President
National Council for Social Studies, 1992-93

Joyce Appleby, President
Organization of American Historians, 1992-1993
Professor of History
University of California, Los Angeles

Samuel Banks, Executive Director
Division of Compensatory and Funded Programs
Baltimore Schools

David Battini, Teacher
Durham High School
Cairo, New York

David Baumbach, Teacher
Woolsair Elementary Gifted Center
Pittsburgh, Pennsylvania

Earl Bell, President
Organization of History Teachers
Teacher, Laboratory Schools
University of Chicago

Mary Bicouvaris, Teacher
Hampton Roads Academy
Newport News, Virginia

Diane Brooks, President,
Council of State Social Studies Specialists, 1993
Manager, California Department of Education

Pedro Castillo, Professor of History
University of California, Santa Cruz

Ainslie T. Embree, Professor of History Emeritus
Columbia University

Elizabeth Fox-Genovese, Professor of History
Emory University

Carol Gluck, Professor of History
Columbia University

Darlene Clark Hine, Professor of History
Michigan State University

Bill Honig, President,
Council of Chief State School Officers, 1992
Distinguished Visiting Professor of Education
San Francisco State University

Akira Iriye, Professor of History
Harvard University

Barbara Talbert Jackson, President
Association for Supervision and
Curriculum Development, 1993-94

Kenneth Jackson, Professor of History
Columbia University

Morton Keller, Professor of History
Brandeis University

Bernard Lewis, Professor of History
Princeton University

William McNeill, Professor of History Emeritus
University of Chicago

Alan D. Morgan, President
Council of Chief State School Officers, 1993
State Superintendent of
Public Instruction, New Mexico

Stephanie Pace-Marshall, President
Association for Supervision and Curriculum
Development, 1992-93

John J. Patrick, Director, Social Studies Development
Center and Professor of Education
Indiana University

Theodore K. Rabb, Chairman
National Council for History Education
Professor of History
Princeton University

C. Frederick Risinger, Associate Director, Social Studies
Development Center and Professor of Education
Indiana University

Denny Schillings, President
National Council for the Social Studies, 1993-94
Teacher, Homewood Flossmoor High School
Flossmoor, Illinois

Gilbert T. Sewall, Director
American Textbook Council

Warren Solomon, Curriculum Consultant for
Social Studies
Missouri Department of Elementary and
Secondary Education

Michael R. Winston, Vice President Emeritus
Howard University and
President, Alfred Harcourt Foundation

Organizational titles of all members were current at the
time of their first participation in the project.

K-4 Curriculum Task Force

David Baumbach, Teacher
Woolsair Elementary Gifted Center
Pittsburgh, Pennsylvania

Charlotte Crabtree, Professor of Education Emeritus
University of California, Los Angeles

Helene Debelak, Teacher
Birchwood Elementary and Junior High School
Cleveland, Ohio

John M. Fisher, Teacher
Fifth Avenue Elementary School
Columbus, Ohio

Marilyn McKnight, Teacher
Forest Home School
Milwaukee, Wisconsin

Lori Lee Morton, Teacher
Riverside Elementary Schools
Alexandria, Virginia

Minna Novick, Curriculum Consultant
Chicago, Illinois

Joan Parrish-Major, Teacher
University Elementary School
University of California, Los Angeles

Sara Shoob, Vice Principal
Cub Run Elementary School
Centreville, Virginia

Linda Symcox, Associate Director
National Center for History in the Schools
University of California, Los Angeles

*Students, West Milford
Township, New Jersey
Photography by Glenn Kamp*

National Forum for History Standards

Ronald Areglado
National Association of Elementary School Principals

Kathy Belter
National Congress of Parents and Teachers

Nguyen Minh Chau
National Association for Asian and
Pacific American Education

Cesar Collantes
League of United Latin American Citizens

Mark Curtis
The Atlantic Council of the United States

Glen Cutlip
National Education Association

Graham Down
Council For Basic Education

Chester E. Finn, Jr.
Educational Excellence Network

Mary Futrell
Quality Education for Minorities Network

Keith Geiger
National Education Association

Ivan Gluckman
National Association of Secondary School Principals

Ruth Granados
Council of the Great City Schools

Joyce McCray
Council for American Private Education

Sr. Catherine T. McNamee
National Catholic Educational Association

Patricia Gordon Michael
American Association for State and Local History

Mabel Lake Murray
National Alliance of Black School Educators

Cynthia Neverdon-Morton
Association for the Study of Afro-American
Life and History

George Nielsen
Lutheran Schools,
The Lutheran Church-Missouri Synod

Charles N. Quigley
Center for Civic Education

Christopher Salter
National Council for Geographic Education

Adelaid Sanford
National Association of State Boards of Education

Albert Shanker
American Federation of Teachers

Ruth Toor
American Association of School Librarians

Clifford Trafzer
Native American Heritage Commission

Hai T. Tran
National Association for Asian and
Pacific American Education

Ruth Wattenberg
American Federation of Teachers

Boy playing Diablo during a
May Day Festival in early 1900s.
Library of Congress

Council of Chief State School Officers
Focus Group

Sue Bennet
California Department of Education

Pasquale DeVito
Rhode Island Department of Education

Patricia Dye, History/Social Studies Consultant
Plymouth, Massachusetts

Mary Fortney
Indiana Department of Education

Connie Manter
Maine Department of Education

Alan D. Morgan
New Mexico State Superintendent of Public Instruction

Wayne Neuburger
Oregon Department of Education

Charles Peters
Oakland Schools, Waterford, Michigan

Thomas Sobol
New York Commissioner of Education

Robert H. Summerville
Alabama Department of Education

Staff
Fred Czarra, Consultant in International Education, Social Studies and Interdisciplinary Learning

Ed Roeber, Director of the State Collaborative on Assessment and Student Standards

Ramsay Selden, Director, State Education Assessment Center

Association for Supervision and Curriculum Development
Focus Group

Glen Blankenship, Social Studies Coordinator
Georgia State Department of Education
Atlanta, Georgia

Joyce Coffey, Teacher
Dunbar Senior High School
District Heights, Maryland

Sherrill Curtiss, Teacher
Chairman, Dept. of History/Social Studies
Providence Senior High School
Charlotte, North Carolina

Geno Flores, Teacher
Arroyo Grande High School
Arroyo Grande, California

Alan Hall, Teacher
Chairman, Social Studies Department
Yarmouth High School
Yarmouth, Massachussetts

Erich Martel, Teacher
Wilson Senior High School
Washington, D.C.

Marilyn McKnight, Teacher
Milwaukee Public Schools
Milwaukee, Wisconsin

Mike Radow, Teacher
Tops Middle School
Seattle, Washington

Karen Steinbrink, Assistant Executive Director
Bucks County Intermediate Unit
Doylestown, Pennsylvania

Staff

Diane Berreth, Deputy Executive Director
Brian Curry, Policy Analyst

National Council for the Social Studies
Focus Group

Linda Levstick, Professor of Education
University of Kentucky

Janna Bremer, Teacher
King Philip Regional High School
Foxborough, Massachusetts

Jean Craven, District Coordinator/Curriculum Devel.
Albuquerque Public School District
Albuquerque, New Mexico

Mathew Downey, Professor of Education
University of California, Berkeley

Rachel Hicks, Teacher
Jefferson Jr. High School
Washington, D.C.

Jack Larner, Coordinator of Secondary
Social Studies, Department of History
Indiana University of Pennsylvania

Tarry Lindquist, Teacher
Lakeridge Elementary
Mercer Island, Washington

Denny Schillings, Teacher
Homewood-Flossmoor High School
Flossmoor, Illinois

Judith S. Wooster, Assistant Superintendent
Bethlehem Central Schools
Del Mar, New York

Ruben Zepeda, Teacher
Grant High School
Van Nuys, California

Council of State Social Studies Specialists
Focus Group

Norman Abramowitz, New York
Margaret (Peggy) Altoff, Maryland
Wendy Bonaiuto, South Dakota
Patricia Boyd, Nevada
Diane L. Brooks, California
Harvey R. Carmichael, Virginia
John M. Chapman, Michigan
Nijel Clayton, Kentucky
Pat Concannon, New Mexico
Edward T. Costa, Rhode Island
Thomas Dunthorn, Florida
Patricia J. Dye, Massachusetts
John D. Ellington, North Carolina
Curt Eriksmoen, North Dakota
Mary Fortney, Indiana
Rita Geiger, Oklahoma
Daniel W. Gregg, Connecticut
Carter B. Hart, Jr., New Hampshire
H. Michael Hartoonian, Wisconsin
Lewis E. Huffman, Delaware
Barbara Jones, West Virginia
Sharon Kaohi, Hawaii
Mary Jean Katz, Oregon
Marianne Kenney, Colorado
Judith Kishman, Wyoming

Frank Klajda, Arizona
John LeFeber, Nebraska
Richard Leighty, Kansas
Constance Miller Manter, Maine
Nancy N. Matthew, Utah
Nanette McGee, Georgia
Marjorie Menzi, Alaska
William Miller, Louisiana
Kent J. Minor, Ohio
John A. Nelson, Vermont
Bruice Opie, Tennessee
Linda Vrooman Peterson, Montana
Barbara Patty, Arkansas
Ann Pictor, Illinois
Joan Prewitt, Mississippi
Orville Reddington, Idaho
Michael Ryan, New Jersey
Warren Solomon, Missouri
Larry Strickland, Washington
Robert Summerville, Alabama
Cordell Svegalis, Iowa
Elvin E. Tyrone, Texas
Margaret B. Walden, South Carolina
Roger Wangen, Minnesota
James J. Wetzler, Pennsylvania

Organization of American Historians
Focus Group

Joyce Appleby, Professor of History
University of California, Los Angeles

Earl Bell, Teacher
The Laboratory Schools
University of Chicago

Alan Brinkley, Professor of History
Columbia University

George Burson, Teacher
Aspen High School
Aspen, Colorado

Albert Camarillo, Professor of History
Stanford University

William H. Chafe, Professor of History
Duke University

Christine L. Compston, Director
History Teaching Alliance
National History Education Network

Terrie L. Epstein, Professor of Education
University of Michigan

Eric Foner, Professor of History
Columbia University

Mary A. Giunta
National Historical Publications and Records Commission
Washington, D.C.

Scott L. Greenwell, Principal
North Layton Junior High
Layton, Utah

David C. Hammack, Professor of History
Case Western Reserve University

Louis R. Harlan, Professor of History
University of Maryland, College Park

George Henry, Jr., Teacher
Highland High School
Salt Lake City, Utah

Marilynn Jo Hitchens, Teacher
Wheat Ridge High School
Denver, Colorado

Michael Kammen, Professor of History
Cornell University

Harvey J. Kaye, Professor of
Social Change and Development
University of Wisconsin, Green Bay

Kathleen C. Kean, Teacher
Nicolet High School
Glendale, Wisconsin

Lawrence W. Levine, Professor of History
University of California, Berkeley

William J. McCracken, Teacher
Pine View School
Sarasota, Florida

Lynette K. Oshima, Professor of Education
University of New Mexico

Pamela Petty, Teacher
Apollo High School
Glendale, Arizona

John Pyne, Humanities Supervisor
West Milford High School
West Milford, New Jersey

Eric Rothschild, Teacher
Scarsdale High School
Scarsdale, New York

Peter Seixas, Professor of Social and
Educational Studies
University of British Columbia

Gloria Sesso, Teacher
Half Hollow Hills High School
Dix Hills, New York

George Stevens, Professor of History
Dutchess Community College
Poughkeepsie, New York

Steven Teel, Teacher
Berkeley High School
Hercules, California

Sandra F. VanBurkleo, Professor of History
Wayne State University

David Vigilante, Teacher Emeritus
Gompers Secondary School
San Diego, California

Bertram Wyatt-Brown, Professor of History
University of Florida

Deborah White, Professor of History
Rutgers University

Mitch Yamasaki, Teacher
Chaminade University of Honolulu
Kaneohe, Hawaii

Charles Anthony Zappia, Professor of History
San Diego Mesa College

Staff

Arnita A. Jones, OAH Executive Director

American Historical Association
U.S. History Focus Group

Albert Camarillo, Professor of History
Stanford University

Terrie Epstein, Professor of Education
University of Michigan

Ned Farman, Teacher
Westtown School
Westtown, Pennsylvania

Elizabeth Faue, Professor of History
Wayne State University

Donald L. Fixico, Professor of History
Western Michigan University

James R. Grossman, Director
Family and Community History Center
Newberry Library
Chicago, Illinois

Louis Harlan, Professor of History
University of Maryland

James O. Horton, Professor of History
George Washington University

Thomas C. Holt, Professor of History
University of Chicago

David Katzman, Professor of History
University of Kansas

Lori Lee Morton, Teacher
Riverside Elementary School
Alexandria, Virginia

Howard Shorr, Teacher
Columbia River High School
Vancouver, Washington

Kathleen Anderson Steeves, Professor of
Education
George Washington University

Staff

James B. Gardner, Acting Executive Director
Noralee Frankel, Assistant Director on Women and
Minorities
Robert B. Townsend, Managing Editor

National Council for History Education
Focus Group

Douglas Greenberg, Chair,
Director, Chicago Historical Society

James Bruggeman, Principal
Irving Elementary School
Bozeman, Montana

Paul H. Fagette, Jr., Professor of History
Arkansas State University

Blythe Hinitz, Professor of Education
Trenton State College

John D. Hoge, Professor of Education
University of Georgia

Arna M. Margolis, Head, History Department
The Bryn Mawr School
Bryn Mawr, Maryland

Richard E. Smith, Teacher
East Corinth Elementary School
Corinth, Mississippi

Jo Sullivan, Principal
Federal Street School
Salem, Massachusetts

Staff
Elaine Reed, Exeutive Secretary

Organization of History Teachers
Focus Group

John Tyler, Chair
Groton School
Groton, Massachusetts

Earl P. Bell, Teacher,
The Laboratory Schools
University of Chicago

Ron Briley, Teacher
Sandia Preparatory School
Albuquerque, New Mexico

Ron Buchheim, Teacher
Dana Hills High School
Dana Point, California

Tom English, Teacher
The George School
Newtown, Pennsylvania

Marianne Gieger, Teacher
Sousa Elementary School
Port Washington, New York

Joe Gotchy, Teacher
Thomas Jefferson High School
West Milford, New Jersey

Paul Horton, Teacher
The Laboratory Schools
University of Chicago

Doris Meadows, Teacher
Wilson Magnet School
Rochester, New York

John M. Pyne, Humanities Supervisor
West Milford High School
West Milford, New Jersey

Robert Rodey, Teacher
Marion Catholic High School
Chicago Heights, Illinois

Gloria Sesso, Teacher
Half Hollow Hills High School
Dix Hills, New York

Peggy Smith, Teacher
St. Mary's High School
Annapolis, Maryland

Richard Swanson, Teacher
The McCallie School
Chattanooga, Tennessee

Art Haycox Elementary School, Oxnard, CA
Photograph by Leticia Zermeno